MW01124454

ADVANCED PUBLISHING AND [...]
STRATEGIES FOR INDIE AUTHORS

SELF-PUBLISHING GUIDE BOOK THREE

Robert J. Ryan

Cover design by 187designz

ISBN: 9781703441352
(print edition)

Trotting Fox Press

P. 18 - GROWING RELEVANCE

P. 44 - CTR PARAMETERS

P. 80 - RYAN'S example METRICS

P. 68 - When TO PAUSE A KeyWORD

Contents

Introduction

Amazon ads are not easy to master. Nothing in indie publishing is. But neglecting to conquer them is a surefire way to see your sales slide and your chance to thrive slip through your fingers.

Why?

Because even if you neglect them, others won't. By others, I mean your competition.

Indie publishing is growing at a rapid rate. What was once an artistic outlet used by a small but budding group is now a full-blown business opportunity for millions to make a profit and a chance for thousands, even tens of thousands, to earn a fulltime living. All over the world, there's a great mass of people working hard, learning the ropes and publishing with skill and knowledge.

Things are harder than they were. They'll get harder still. Once, Amazon gave visibility in their store for free. Now, they charge for it.

It's that simple. Amazon ads are not the only way to get visibility and sales, but they're a good way. If you leave them alone, others won't. They'll learn their uses and master them. With that advantage, they'll climb above you.

What it comes down to, one way or another, is that in order to sell you need to drive traffic to your books. If they don't get seen, they don't get bought.

Amazon ads drive traffic to your books. More than that, they drive customers to your books who are willing to pay full price. Newsletter promotions, Countdown Deals and BookBub ads don't do that. Facebook ads can, but your competitors will be using them, too.

Eventually, you'll want to master Facebook ads. But Amazon ads are easier to grasp, and they have advantages Facebook ads can't offer.

This book will give you the knowledge you need to compete with the masses. More, it will give you the knowledge to *outcompete* them.

This isn't a beginner's book. If you're looking for the basics of how to get started, there are plenty of free resources on the internet to show you. Not to mention books and courses.

So, what *is* this book then?

This is an all-in-one *advanced* guide to mastering Amazon ads by a six-figure author who makes his living from writing and advertising his books. It'll reveal hard-won truths, and save you years of effort and wasted money.

I offered some advice in books one and two of the series. *All the hard work in the world isn't enough. That labor must be guided by correct knowledge, or the effort is lost.*

That advice holds true for this book. When you finish, tell me if you think I've given you that knowledge.

1. The Strategies of Advertising

I say *strategies* in the chapter title for a reason. There's more than one when it comes to Amazon ads, and we'll look closely at each.

Failing to determine your exact strategy is a key reason for failing at ads. Following advice from an industry adviser who works to a different strategy than suits your circumstances is catastrophic.

And the shoe fits on the other foot, too. Giving advice as though there was only one way to do things and one purpose is just as bad.

Both happen. A lot.

But the purpose of advertising is to make a profit, right?

That's too vague. That's too wishy-washy. It doesn't dig deep enough for success. And, if you've been reading this series from book one, you know that's the motto. Dig deep. Find the truth. Question standard practice – seek *best* practice.

When we apply that mindset to Amazon ads, we find that there are four different strategies. You'll see these four at play if you stalk, I mean study, successful authors and how they advertise.

You may not know what a successful author thinks, but you sure can see what they're doing. Look at their ads. Where on Amazon are they advertising? What products are they advertising on? How high up the Sponsored Product carousel are they?

All these things give you a good idea of how big their advertising budget is and how much they're bidding. Most of all, they tell you what strategy they're following.

So, back to the point. Can Amazon ads be run for profit? You bet. Each of the four strategies has the ultimate goal of profit. But they get there in four entirely different ways.

Which one will work for you?

Small-scale profit

This is the strategy of the beginner. It's how to proceed when you're learning the ropes and coming to grips with how Amazon ads work.

It's also the strategy of those who have no long series, boxed set or large backlist.

The goal here is to advertise books and learn how to make a profit off those ads. It doesn't matter if the clicks and conversions add up slowly. They can take weeks or months to accrue. In the end, if you've mastered this strategy, you'll turn $10.00 a month into $12.00, or something like that. You'll have a trickle of extra sales above organic levels. Life is sweet because you're making a profit even if it's small.

But it sure isn't any get rich quick scheme. It's slow and steady. It's also low maintenance.

I mentioned three important points above. *Long series*. *Boxed set*. And *large backlist*.

Not having these (or at least a very large standalone) is the limiting factor here. Without them, you're forced into lower budgets, lower bids and consequently a lower volume of impressions.

There's no way around this. Even if your books convert well (and we'll go into conversions later) you need impressions to get clicks. And you need clicks to get conversions. It's that simple.

This is neither a good thing nor a bad thing. It's just reality. Budget and bid amounts are like a water tap. They allow you to turn on the water. In this case, the water is a stream of impressions. If you can only turn the tap a tiny bit, you only get a dribble of water.

A long series, boxed sets, a large backlist and a good conversion rate enable you to turn that tap around and around.

Writers fall into four main groups here. Those who choose to write in a long series. Those who choose not to. Those who are happy to, but haven't because they didn't realize the significance of the choice. And those who have only just started publishing, or thinking about it.

I don't judge you whatever applies. Whichever camp you're in, it's your business and you have your reasons. You should know the consequences of those choices though.

If you can't turn on the tap, the best you can do with Amazon ads (and any other ads) is a slow trickle. And even that will be hard.

There are other ways to get visibility besides ads. For instance, permafree. But those methods work better with ads too.

In short, the small-scale profit model is certainly doable. But it's very hard. Choose it if your artistic spirit refuses to bow to commercial pressures (and you won't get more commercial than competing for visibility to sell on Amazon) or as a preparation to learn the ropes so that as your publishing career expands you're ready to move onto different advertising strategies.

Whatever you chose, whichever camp you fit into, the rest of the information in this book about how ads work will position you to make the most of your specific situation.

For what it's worth, my personal choice is to write in a longer series. My genre is epic fantasy, which is the true home of trilogies, and trilogies is what I've mostly released. But readers love a five-book series, or more, just as much. That's the direction I've moved to, and it's worked for me. It's a business decision (because I'm a fulltime writer) but it doesn't disturb my artistic side in the least.

But that's me. What you do is your choice. I'm just making sure you've got the information at your disposal so you can make an informed decision.

Having made that decision, make sure you apply the correct advertising strategy. If you only have a few books, and they're not in a series, following some of the other strategies will torch your money.

If you're following advice from an industry source, make sure their advice isn't one-size-fits-all. If it is, that's a warning bell, and I suggest you run like a gold-laden cargo ship fleeing the Black Pearl…

Higher-scale profit

This is a strategy for when your published material lets you start turning the tap. Impressions are the foundation of success with Amazon ads. By themselves, they're meaningless, but in tandem with advanced optimization tactics, they're the raw material of victory.

We'll talk about optimization later. Enough to say here that skillful optimization is like adjusting water quality. Your tap can gush muddy, bacteria-infested water straight from a dam, or purified water – fresh and ready to drink.

To utilize this strategy you'll need what's lacking in the first: a long series or a boxed set. You may also have a large backlist and a good conversion rate. If so, your results will be even better.

There's a myth that a click is a click is a click. People who've never been taught how to optimize properly tend to believe in it. The theory proposes that no matter the source of the click, once you have it then you have the same chance of converting as any other click. This, proponents of the theory say, allows you to reap greater profit because you can target low-quality click sources, and do it cheaply. It's a quantity over quality scenario.

I'll have more to say on that in the optimization segments of this book. For now, think on this. If that theory were correct, conversion rates of different ads would all end up similar.

And they don't. Talk to anyone who ever runs PPC ads and ask them if conversion rates for different ads are the same, and listen to them laugh.

The click is a click is a click theory is wrong. Nor is it supported by genuine PPC experts.

As always in this series, I encourage you never to take anything at face value. Research and verify. A good starting point on this topic is a Google search for "Why PPC conversion rates differ" or "How can I improve my ad conversion rate?"

Look for articles by people who run PPC businesses professionally.

This myth, widely propagated in some indie author circles but non-existent in all other fields of PPC advertising (Facebook ads, Google ads, and even Amazon sellers of products besides books) is killing you. Big time.

Don't take my word for it. Take nobody's word for anything. Search and verify. Find the confirming patterns.

What has any of this got to do with the subject at hand of higher-scale profit?

When your ads are optimized properly, you have a higher conversion rate and this means you *spend less* to get a sale. Each click that doesn't convert costs you money. Clicks that do convert make you money. When you tilt the balance in your favor, you're *profiting*.

Better still, optimizing allows you to bid higher. The money you save by not paying for low-converting ads can be redirected to high-converting ads. This turns on the tap and enables you to start scaling up.

The click is a click is a click theory requires low bids over wide targets to work. This tries to make up for low conversion rates. But it turns off your ability to truly scale. You only get what you pay for, and if you bid low you can't successfully target quality keywords that convert well and at volume.

You can optimize with the small-scale profit strategy too. In fact, that's key to making it work. But without the leverage of a long series or the like, you still can't turn on the tap. Turning on the tap enables you to find a good thing and make it better, stronger, faster.

Okay, that was a retro reference. Fans of the *Six Million Dollar Man* will have gotten it. But the reference is apt. Optimization of ads for a book you can leverage to sell more books is the strategy for higher-scale profit. Your ads will perform better.

Breaking even brings better profit

So far so good. The two previous strategies are acceptable. There's nothing wrong with them, assuming you want to profit from your ads.

But there's another option. And it's better still. It turns the *Six Million Dollar Man* into the *Six Billion Dollar Man*. Or maybe even Chris Hemsworth.

10

I said earlier that you have to dig deeper and "profit" was too wishy-washy an aim. Here is the proof of it. Be warned though, this section is one of the most complex in the book. I could leave it out, but that would be doing you a disservice. You deserve to know the truth, or at least the truth as I see it.

What's better? Profiting off your ads? Or profiting off your books?

The key to arriving at an answer here is an understanding of the Amazon ecosystem. Amazon reward sales, and they punish a lack of sales. They do this because they always put the customer first, and try to show them what they're most likely to buy.

Amazon's recommendation engine is vast and multifaceted. And it never rests. Whenever the customer is there, it's there. If you sell in a tiny way, just a book a week, that recommendation engine works in a tiny way. If you sell in a big way, the floodgates open and the recommendation engine promotes you everywhere. It's like a politician at election time. It's kissing babies, making speeches, smiling and shaking hands without stint.

What exactly *is* the recommendation engine though? Amazon sends millions of emails a day to subscribers. Millions. Then there's the "also-bought", "also-viewed" and "what other items do customers buy after viewing this" item rows. These are the main ones, but there are others. These all form the working cogs of the engine.

If you start a trickle of sales, the recommendation engine responds. Where there's one, there's the other. If you're advertising, and getting sales off your ads, then you're getting sales off the recommendation engine too.

And this is the interesting part. Obviously, there's a lot of variation, but authors often report that only about 30% of their revenue comes directly from ads. That means 70% of their income comes from organic sales.

This certainly matches my personal experience, and it matches what Amazon sellers of products other than books also report.

The use of this information? Ads are a lever. Sales from ads stimulate organic sales through the recommendation engine. And organic sales are roughly double ad sales.

This is why you generally *don't* want to profit off your ads. Going to the break-even point instead puts more pressure on the lever. This extra pressure boosts organic sales even further, where you make more money than you do off ads.

If you can run break-even ads, the risk of this strategy is extremely low. You're running a cost-neutral scenario on the ads, and bringing in sales organically. Should you choose to, you can push it a bit further by running ads at a slight loss, so long as they still convert really well.

When you're in the break-even situation, what you want to do is scale as high as possible. But scaling is very, very hard. For this reason, I give it its own chapter later.

This is where things get even more complex. Some of you have been taught that the way to measure profit from your ads is to subtract ad costs from total income. The balance is your profit, generated by ads.

This method is problematic and pays no attention to organic sales. It ignores them. But let me ask you this. If you can run an ad on Amazon that sells your book, why won't people buy the same book when Amazon recommends it via also-boughts, emails and the like?

The truth is, they *do* buy it. But you need to stimulate that recommendation engine first. You can switch on ads in hours. You can switch them off in seconds. The recommendation engine can take weeks to ramp up. But once you get it going, it chugs along very consistently. But if you turn off your ads, it will begin to stall. *Or not.* It depends on how well the book resonates and sells organically.

How many of you have kept paying for ads and keywords that were losing you money because organic sales were coming in separately and being falsely attributed to the ads?

Attributing *all* profits to ads and ignoring organic sales prevents you from working out which ads, and the keywords within them, are duds. Why optimize when they all *seem* to be working well?

This approach will cost you money, either by a small amount or by the truckload. And if you learned it from a book or course, ask yourself this question. Is it in the interests of the author or teacher that their methods appear as successful as possible? If your answer is yes, then from their point of view, attributing *all* sales to ads makes a certain kind of sense. Yes?

The justification put forward for calculating ad effectiveness this way is that Amazon's reporting of ad sales is unreliable. This claim has gained currency. There are certainly some issues if your book is enrolled in Kindle Unlimited because page reads generated by ads aren't captured after the 14-day attribution window. The volume of page reads after 14 days would be small, though. As for sales? I don't think the reporting is unreliable at all. I believe it's laser accurate. If Amazon can land a book at your front door by drone, I think they know when someone clicked an ad and bought a book. And directors would face possible jail time for fraud if they deliberately provided dodgy sales figures.

What do you think?

All through this series, I have a motto. Dig deep. Find the truth. Question standard practice – seek *best* practice. Digging deeper now, I suggest that there are three layers of sales going on in the Amazon ecosystem.

The first you can attribute *directly* to the ads that are working. Not all will be, especially in a cost-effective way. Nobody creates a bunch of ads that all work. Even PPC experts who run campaigns for multimillion-dollar companies. They're happy if seven out of ten ads work.

The second layer you can attribute *indirectly* to the ads. Because the ads lifted sales rank, they kickstarted the recommendation engine. Or, if you have a mailing list and a good release strategy, they gave an increased boost to what was already happening.

The third layer is actual, real, genuine, organic sales. Depending on where you are in your career and the number of fans you have, these sales can make up a small portion or a very, very large portion of your total sales.

Attributing that third layer of sales as profit from your ads is artificially inflating their performance. Doing so causes you to keep poorly performing ads that are siphoning off your cash like a petrol thief in the dead of night.

But what of the indirect layer? Those sales come about because of the ads. It was the ads after all that lifted your sales rank and caused Amazon to start sending out emails with your book in it, or increase the emails they were already sending out.

This is a good point. I don't disagree with it. But if you're running ten ads, which ads were responsible for this and which weren't? If each ad has a hundred keywords in it, again, which ones are good and which ones duds?

The central word here is *indirectly*. Can we pin things down better than that and optimize profits in a targeted way instead of generalize by subtracting expenses from income?

Yes we can.

The direct cause of starting or increasing recommendations is sales rank. When this goes up, the recommendations increase. When this goes down, the recommendations decrease.

To work out which ads are responsible for this, you have to analyze them and pinpoint which ones influence the sales rank in a cost-effective manner. This can be done. It can be done fairly easily, and doing so will allow you to delete dud ads and keywords.

This, in turn, allows you to direct more money toward effective ads and keywords instead of funding them all, winners and losers alike.

We'll go into how to calculate ad performance in detail shortly. For the moment, it's back to the core strategies.

Investing in loss

The small-scale strategy presented first doesn't enable you to use ads to lever the recommendation engine. The sales generated by the ads are too few to have much impact on the algorithms. The second higher-scale strategy gets the ball rolling. It moves the lever, and the recommendation engine switches on. It increases your profits over and above the ads.

With the third strategy of breaking even, the magic of Amazon ads truly begins.

But to succeed as an indie publisher, you need to think strategically. And you can never take anything at face value. Methods and tactics must be considered, verified, tested and discarded – or adopted as appropriate. Not all advice is good. Not all good techniques will work for everyone.

Find what's best for you, but always seek to change gears to move up to a higher speed. This keeps you ahead of your competition. If you're on strategy one, consider how you can get to strategy two. If you're sitting on strategy two, consider moving to strategy three.

But the fourth strategy is potentially the most profitable of all. It's also the riskiest. For that reason, it's not for everyone. I include it here because this is an advanced book. You'll see this strategy at play on the tops of bestseller lists if you study them carefully.

Is it for you? That's for you to decide. I wouldn't try it until you've mastered the first three. This gives you the background knowledge to apply it best. It also gives you the confidence to pull the hardest strategy of all off. And you *do* need confidence for this strategy. You want to know before you begin that your books resonate with the target audience. You want to know that they convert well.

There are two main ways this invest-in-loss strategy works. This is the first.

You have a new release. It's either book one of a long series, and several further books in this series are already written and available for rapid release at, say, two-week intervals. Or you have a fairly large box set.

And, as I said above, you have confidence born of experience that your books *sell*.

Then you release. As you do so, you apply a range of promotional activities as per normal. You'll use your mailing list. You might price at 99 cents temporarily. You'll probably have a bunch of Facebook or BookBub campaigns going. Overarching everything, you have Amazon ads running.

And you don't budget and bid to break even. You go higher than that. Especially, *most especially*, with Amazon ads.

All these things together are working to give you momentum. They're giving you the best possible shot at a good sales rank. The lower the better, but you have to hold it there for at least five days. Ten would be better.

The recommendation engine pricks its ears and gets to work like a border collie rounding up sheep. Your book is in also-boughts and emails. It's on Hot New Release lists and Bestseller lists. It's everywhere, and it has momentum.

It's also costing you money to promote. You're spending a *lot* at this point. It can be difficult to make a profit even with bids of, say, 60 cents. But you're not after profit just at this point.

You're after steady sales at a great sales rank. People in this phase bid as high as $2.00 to $5.00. Some even higher.

It's worth reminding you at this point that bid price is not the cost per click. CPC is sometimes 20 to 30% lower.

After five to ten days you adjust all promotions and ads back to break-even levels. This pretty much means stopping everything except Facebook and Amazon ads because they're the only ones that have the potential to run at profit or break-even points.

I said to adjust things to break even, but I meant with one exception. Keep your Amazon ads running at high bids. Turn off ads and keywords that aren't working, but leave the ones that convert well as they are for the moment, even if they still run at a large loss.

What does all this achieve?

The answer comes in two parts. First, you achieve momentum in the store. Your book is everywhere. If it resonates, it'll stick. It'll keep that great rank for a long time. The slide down the lists will be slow instead of fast. For weeks or months or even a year, your book will generate great revenue. You'll have operated at a loss for a few weeks. Perhaps a big loss of several thousand dollars. But, if the strategy works for you, you'll earn that money back in short order and then ride a wave of profit for a long time afterward.

The second part is this. Amazon ads do something that no other ads can do.

It's called seeding. I discussed it in the first book of this series. What is it?

Relevance is a huge factor in Amazon ads. We'll go into details later, but for now it's enough to know that Amazon rewards relevance and punishes irrelevance. This is part of their customer-centric approach. They always try to put books in front of people that they want to buy.

And you can actively grow relevance by advertising a book on a free or 99-cent promo via Amazon ads on highly targeted products. This works better than full price because click through is higher and conversion rates are at least double. Getting clicks, and converting, again and again, off a keyword shows Amazon that your book is relevant to that keyword. So they give that book preference over less relevant books. Or equally relevant books at a higher price that don't convert as well because of the price. You get better ad placement higher up the carousel and for a cheaper cost per click.

Alternatively, if you don't convert, it costs more to get lesser ad placement. In this way Amazon encourages advertisers to put books in front of customers that the customers want to see.

This, like the rest of the strategy, comes with an upfront financial loss. But in exchange you obtain greater relevance and consequently lower costs per click and better ad placement over your competitors. To pull it off though, be sure to target well. If you don't, your gains will be quickly eroded by low conversion rates after the launch promotion finishes.

There you have it. BookBub and Facebook ads can't build relevance. For that reason, I suggest you fund Amazon ads to a higher level than the other options. Keep that funding going while you continue to discount the book, and then switch to full price and reoptimize your ads so they work toward the break-even point again.

There's another thing to note here. People often talk about discovery ads where they identify good and bad

18

keywords. When they have a bunch of good keywords, they kill off the old ads and start new ones with just those.

This will probably hurt you. It'll especially hurt you if you've built up relevance.

Why?

Because you lose that relevance when you start a new ad. You lose it like it never existed. This concept goes against what many people teach about advertising books. They say ads die and you need to kill them off and start new ones. Or find all your good keywords and put them together. My advice is this. *Never* kill an ad or keyword that's working.

This is what Amazon themselves have to say in their help pages.

When you copy a campaign, you essentially create a new one, and it behaves as if it has no previous performance history (which is a key input used by Amazon's algorithms to identify the optimal bid under dynamic bidding) – so the original campaign will have an unfair advantage over the copied one.

I could wish Amazon gave us a more transparent insight into how their ads work, but that's pretty clear. Copied ads don't piggyback performance history with them. Does this apply to new ads? There's no reason to think it doesn't.

So if a keyword or ad is working, don't copy it or start new ads. If it ain't broke, don't fix it. Just delete those parts that aren't working, and keep the rest.

I have to advise again that this last strategy is potentially highly rewarding (it's worked great for me) but it's also risky. Very risky. I'm not recommending it, but merely showing you the strategies at play on the Amazon marketplace. Don't even think about trying the strategy unless you know that your books generally sell well and you can absorb the loss if it doesn't work.

But now that you know how it works, keep an eye out for it. You'll see it being employed again and again. Watch the authors who do it. Study their methods. Observe how long they discount. Estimate their ad costs. Estimate their profit or loss during the launch phase, and then a month later. Keep watching and estimating for several months. Then decide if the strategy is for you.

There's another variation on this strategy. Again, if you look, you'll see it at play frequently. It goes like this.

Take a boxed set enrolled in the Kindle Unlimited program, and preferably a large one close to the 3000-page KENPC limit. It might be an old or a new release, but it works much better new. Price it at 99 cents and advertise it heavily with Amazon ads.

Conversion rates here are about one for every five clicks, which is very high. But again, this depends greatly on how well the book resonates with the target audience.

Conversions on a boxed set priced about $7.99 tend to run at about one sale to two full page reads. Dropping to 99 cents mixes this up. At such a bargain price, most people buy now instead of borrow. But you'll still get some borrows, and these pay at the normal rate per page read.

This is not a scenario in which you can profit from the ads.

Not *directly*. But that's not the strategy. Once again, it relies on obtaining a good sales rank. A great sales rank is better. Even royalties on a 99-cent price point rack up if you sell thirty or more a day. More importantly, the page reads creep up as the rank drops.

Assuming the book resonates, it *will* climb steeply in the ranks. It gets the recommendation engine all excited like a kid at Christmas who still believes in Santa, and you have a hit.

The ads spur organic sales. Organic sales and ads combined improve relevancy on keywords that convert and Amazon gives your ads more oxygen. Everything is spurring the sales rank, including that you populate high on the also-boughts of bestselling books, themselves with great sales rank, giving you free visibility. And the page reads pour in.

This can turn a seeming loss into a profit. When the dust settles down, optimize the ads as best as possible, but expect them to run at a loss. That is, until you factor in the page reads indirectly spurred by increased visibility and the recommendation engine.

Just keep in mind that the ratio of sales to borrows increases when you lower the book price.

This strategy has another benefit. It grows your mailing list. This will translate into extra sales in the future. Not everything is about profit in the here and now. Look at the big picture, and look to the future.

Again, this is a risky strategy. I'm not advising it, but merely showing you what's possible and what happens in the marketplace. Once again, study the authors doing this. I shouldn't say it, but books like the one you're reading now are a poor substitute. The best teachers are the strategies and tactics at play in the marketplace, if only you stop to observe the secrets in plain sight.

There you have it. These are the four main strategies of Amazon ads.

Keep in mind which strategy applies to you now, or that you may want to move up to, as we go through what follows. Also keep it in mind whenever and wherever someone gives advice or comments on Amazon ads. Filter their advice through your strategy to see if it applies to what *you're* doing, or if it's advice for a different strategy that will harm you if you try to implement it out of place.

2. How Expert Advertisers Target

I've touched on the differences between targeting at low bids and targeting at higher bids. Now's the time to dig deeper into that.

Impression volume is turning on the tap. You need to get impressions first in order to get clicks. And you need clicks in order to get conversions.

One strategy to gain impression volume is to target as widely as possible. The more ads you have, weighed down with keywords like a monkey scampering away from a banana plantation, the more impressions you get.

So far so good. Amazon caters for this. Should you wish, you can run category ads.

In my case, I might run an epic fantasy category ad. This targets all books listed in the category. That's a lot. A whopping lot. There're enough bananas there to feed an army of rampaging monkeys. The potential impression volume is massive to the power of ten.

But I write traditional-style epic fantasy. The category, though, is a mixed bag of other things. First, there's grimdark versus noblebright – the more traditional flavor of epic fantasy. People tend to read one or the other. Much less often they read both. So, in a category ad, my noblebright books are being shown indiscriminately to grimdark readers. And those folks are numerous.

I'll get impressions here, and lots of them, but those grimdark readers won't convert well on my books.

But things get worse. Extremely popular just at the moment in the Amazon store is reverse-harem fantasy. It should have its own category, but it gets lumped in with epic fantasy. My mind boggles at what Tolkien would have thought of that, but I digress.

And if reverse harem isn't enough, litrpg fiction (literary role playing game fiction, which again should have its own category) is thrown in with epic fantasy too.

There are other things in this mixed bag as well. For instance, character driven versus plot driven stories and epic fantasy romance.

My noblebright book ad could be shown on all these books in a category ad. It (potentially) gets a massive impression volume, but perhaps only twenty percent of the impressions are on similar noblebright books. And that's where the readers I want to reach are mostly hanging out.

I said *potentially* massive impressions. But I have to win the bid auction first to be a chance of being seen.

And who am I bidding against? Authors of grimdark fantasy. Authors of litrpg books and of epic fantasy romance. I'm competing against them, but for what? To be seen on something like a grimdark book where, for the most part, my audience doesn't hang out.

Even if I win the auction, I lose. My target audience isn't there. Impressions that don't have the potential to turn into conversions are wasting everyone's time.

The shoe fits on the other foot too. Authors of grimdark are in the same boat, bidding to try to win auctions for visibility on a reverse harem book. Reverse harem authors are … you get the picture.

If you believe in the click is a click is a click theory, you're waving your hands around for attention right now. Yes, I know, and you're right. On Amazon ads, we don't pay for *impressions* but for *clicks*. This means that all those wasted impressions are irrelevant. It's only a click we pay for, and if someone clicks that means we've found someone who's interested in our book.

You're right. Some of the time. Just because someone's looking at a reverse harem book doesn't mean they don't read epic fantasy. If they do, and they see my book and click, they might buy.

But not everyone who clicks studies the title, cover and blurb-snippet first. They're on a reverse harem book. Most of the books in the also-bought carousel will be reverse harem books. *The background expectation of that customer is that the things they're seeing on that page relate to reverse harem.*

Click. How long do people study ads before they click? Click. Not long. Click. People have trigger fingers. Click. Clicking is easy, and back-clicking is too when their internet surfing takes them in a direction they don't want to go.

Advertisers pay for these clicks. And they pay for them with no chance of a conversion. Really, the click is a click is a click theory makes me sick to my stomach. People often bleed money because they've been taught PPC advertising by the inept and clueless.

This is why well-targeted ads have higher click through *and* conversion rates.

Of course, not all broad-targeted clicks are wasted. I could be advertising a nonfiction book about curing back pain on an Agatha Christie novel. Or on a reverse harem book. Or on a how-to-date guide. I'm going to get a portion of "false expectation" clicks, but anyone, no matter their reading preferences, can suffer from back pain.

That situation is a genuine click with a genuine chance of conversion. But the idea of targeting is to stack the deck in your favor. The more you do that, the better you can convert. The higher your conversion rate, the higher you can bid. This turns on the tap. You get a bigger stream of highly targeted and higher converting clicks.

This is why broad targeting uses low bids. Most clicks don't convert, so the bid has to be low to try to make up the difference in sheer volume of impressions.

It can work. Occasionally. When it does, it's usually for a nonfiction book that has broad appeal to a wide range of the population. In fiction, it tends to work better for thrillers and romance, because they're the most widely read genres.

On the whole though, broad targeting is torching your money.

Try it, and see if it works for you. You may have a book that resonates across a wide audience. Study your click-through rate. Study your conversion rate. See if you can break even this way.

Few can. If you're one of them, go with it.

As an aside, it's worth noting that not all categories are as messed up as epic fantasy. If you have a homogenous category, where the majority of books are actually fairly similar, broad targeting may work. But most categories are as bad or worse than epic fantasy.

So far, we've really covered a what-not-to-do scenario. In general, poor targeting gives poor results. The better you target, the better your results.

Category ads are about as broad as you can get. Refining that down, you can start to target by genre. This requires manual entry of keywords when setting up the ad. You have to find keywords that match your book's genre.

This tends to produce better results. You can match romance to romance, epic fantasy to epic fantasy, dystopian to dystopian etc.

Like I say, this will likely give you better results. But that doesn't mean good results or break-even results.

People don't really read by genre. They read by subgenre. Expectation is still just as much at play as it was before. Someone looking at a billionaire-bad-boy book has an expectation that an ad on that book's page is going to be for something similar. If the ad takes them to a second-chance romance, there's still a high likelihood of a disconnect.

That's not to say that some readers don't like both types of books. But PPC advertising is a numbers game. The more numbers you can herd into your corner, the bigger your army. The more deserters you have, the smaller your army.

And the bigger army generally wins. What loses is thinking you have a big army (lots of impressions and clicks) when in reality you're paying a fortune for food and equipment for deserters who aren't even there.

Expectation is a big thing. It's been discussed in previous books in the series in relation to copywriting that the human brain doesn't really like to think. Thinking takes energy and effort. And most of the time it's not necessary. Instinct, learned behavior patterns and unconscious decision-making shape most of our everyday actions rather than rigorous analysis.

You don't need to think of it in order to breathe. Or walk. Or tie your shoelaces.

Here's another way to look at it. This is a series of numbers.

Two.
Four.
Six.

What's the next number in that list?

It's eight, isn't it? Of course, in theory, it could be any number, for instance five. This would have created a pattern of a three-letter number followed by a four-letter number. There were no rules. But your brain was lulled into the more obvious pattern, took the easy route, and an expectation was formed. For those interested, this is what neuroscientists call the adaptive unconscious. It makes decisions behind your back.

Back to books. The concept is no different when a prospective buyer is browsing the Amazon store. They've clicked on a book cover of a certain type. The blurb reinforced it was that type of book. But maybe it's too expensive and they don't buy it. They click on an also-bought. It, too, is the same type of book. The pattern has formed and been reinforced. But they realize they've read this a year ago. Then they see a cover that stands out in the ad carousel, and click it. They're now on your book.

You've paid for that click. But on reading the blurb, the prospect realizes it's for steamy romance and not the sweet romance they were looking for. Or it's grimdark fantasy rather than noblebright fantasy. Or it's … you get the drift.

You've paid for the click, but you were never going to get the sale. Now, repeat the process with customer after customer. Every once in a while, you might find a clicker who reads more widely. You'll get some sales. But, generally, not enough to break even. Often, you're torching money.

Customer expectation counts. It counts big time. But the good news? You can flip this on its head. You can make those expectations work for you instead of against you.

How do you do this?

You do it with targeting. You do it with laser-like targeting. You find those patterns and you make sure your book is an *eight*.

Subgenre is one of the patterns. When picking your targets, look for the patterns that match. Is your cover similar to the target's cover? And the blurb? Does this give off a similar vibe in terms of story? Is the age of the hero similar? Their sex? Does it look like a plot-based book or a character-based book? What about the style of writing? Does it belong to a long series, while yours is a standalone?

You're looking for similarities on all these points. You don't have to be identical though. If that were the case, you could never target anything but your own book.

Are there other patterns? Yes. Is the author male or female? Often, female authors are read by females and male authors by men. If you doubt this, pick some female authors at random and look at who predominantly leaves them reviews. It'll mostly be females. The same applies for men (but not as much).

For sure, there are exceptions. A lot of them. If in doubt, look at the names of the reviewers. That will tell you if you're dealing with one or not.

There are still more patterns. Buyers of traditionally published books tend to buy traditionally published books. Buyers of indie books tend to buy indie books. Again, confirm this by looking at the also-boughts of the book in question.

This is how you refine targeting to highly optimized levels. This is how you weed out keywords that will drain your budget for little benefit.

Choose your target keywords wisely. Fit to the pattern. This increases your conversion rate and allows you to bid high enough to get more impressions. And in this case, turning on the tap brings you a stream of not just impressions but of conversions.

Don't take my word for this stuff. Put it to the test. Run comparison ads along the lines above. Trial it. You'll find that the closer you meet the pattern of expectation the higher CTR and conversion rate you get.

When this fails, it's gold. Go back and look at the patterns. You *thought* everything matched, and you got a high CTR (indicating high prospect interest) but ended up with low conversions.

Why?

Something in the pattern *didn't* match. This is how you learn nuances even within your own subgenre that you've been reading and writing in for years. Those nuances matter. Targeting matters. Expectations matter.

Targeting wide is guessing.

Don't guess. *Know.*

When you have one or more laser-targeted ads working well and making a profit or breaking even (depending on your strategy) then you can try to expand. Start some ads on keywords that don't quite meet the pattern of your book, but where there may be crossover. Prepare for many of these ads to fail, but not all of them will.

3. Purifying the Gold

I'm going to digress briefly. But when I come back to the subject of targeting, you'll see it in an even clearer light. Much will make sense that didn't before. And the reason many of your ads fail will be clearer too.

In book one I discussed how there's a war being fought between Amazon and the Big Five traditional publishers. It's covert at the moment, unlike a few years ago. Back then, the US Government filed a suit against Apple and the Big Five publishers alleging they conspired to illegally raise and fix the price of ebooks sold via Amazon. The publishers settled, but Apple went to court. A big mistake, I guess, because they ended up having to pay $450 million.

Ouch. Settling and massive payouts hurt. And behind it all is the legacy model of publishing. Investors in that model *don't* want it to die out and give way to the digital model as has happened in the music, newspaper and magazine worlds.

But the war never stopped. It's just legal now, and underground. And as I said in book one, Amazon is silently winning it. Their tactics are listed there, so I'm not going to repeat them.

But one of those tactics bears directly on Amazon ads. I said earlier that people who buy traditionally published books tend to predominantly buy traditionally published books. The same applies to indie buyers. Likewise, paperbacks and ebooks.

People buy by habit. They're invested in one way of doing things, or another. Neuroscience calls this "priors".

Of course, there's crossover. But not a great deal. Look at the also-boughts for proof of this.

How does this impact Amazon ads? How does it influence targeting and conversions?

Like this. If you're an indie and you target a popular author in your subgenre by either author name or book title, which are both generally advised things to do, your ebook ad will display on either ebooks or paperbacks, probably both, and *entirely* at Amazon's discretion.

But buyers browsing Amazon's Book Store (dominated by traditional publishers) mostly aren't ebook buyers. If they were, they'd be browsing in the Kindle Store.

About half the impressions you get come from such a scenario, and are mostly wasted. You were never much chance of getting a sale. The same applies to the clicks, if you keep in mind my previous comments about expectations.

But Amazon are nevertheless happy to display your ebook ad on paperback titles.

Why?

Because they're trying to tempt paperback buyers away from traditionally published books and into the Kindle Store, which is dominated by indies. When you advertise an ebook on a paperback, Amazon is using your money to promote the Kindle Store to paperback buyers and win further market share from the Big Five. The end goal is to *destroy* traditional publishing. At least, I think so.

It's not a creative tactic. It's employed in business all the time. By way of example, real estate agents use a variation of it frequently. Most home buyers are sourced from close proximity to the house for sale. Most buyers find houses they're interested in via an actual for sale sign on a local road they use or by one of the internet databases. Yet real estate agents often talk clients into advertising in statewide newspapers. Sadly, these ads are not really to sell the home. The agents use the opportunity (and someone else's money) to promote their *brand* to the widest audience possible.

Clever. Effective. But not very nice. Then again, no one ever said business was going to be a morning tea with pigs in a blanket and marzipan brownies.

Back to Amazon. Multiply the process of displaying ebook ads on paperback books over countless titles and a period of years, and the strategy is effective. But not for the individual advertiser. For them, it translates into lower click through and conversion rates.

All this is why an ad can seem to work for a while and then falter. Amazon may have showed it against ebooks initially, then started padding out impressions on paperback books. This gets you hooked on ad performance in the beginning, and then you always live in hope that the higher conversion rate will return. While you live in hope, you keep funding that ad.

My strategy for dealing with all of this? I rarely target keywords by either author name or book title anymore. Not even other indie authors, although the situation is not as bad with them as with traditionally published authors. I target my Sponsored Product ads by selecting the product targeting option and then the individual products option, pasting in ASIN numbers of my target ebooks from a master list. This gets me off paperbacks and displays my ad solely on the relevant ebooks.

Finding highly relevant ASIN numbers, and copying and pasting them into a master list takes a lot of effort. But the results are worth it. This list is then ready to paste into new ads for new books when they're released. Be sure to keep it updated though.

The strategy reduces impressions. But these were ineffective paperback impressions. My average click-through rate is now under 1 in 500. Generally, advisers are happy with 1 in 1000. And I have many keywords that produce 1 in 100. Conversions, being buys and borrows, regularly (but not always) come in at 1 in 5 clicks.

As always, don't take my word for any of this. They're only theories until you prove them to your own satisfaction. Try my way, and see if it doesn't greatly improve CTR and conversion rate.

You can do the opposite experiment too. Start up an ad for an ebook and target it to *paperbacks* by using the method above, except flip the ASIN numbers for ISBN numbers. See what happens. For most of you, probably all of you, you'll sell a majority of paperbacks and few ebooks. Your ACOS will look good on paper, but in a true comparison of expense to profit you'll probably be making a loss. More importantly, those sales do nothing to boost organic sales of ebooks. It is, however, a way to increase your paperback sales. Just be sure that you're breaking even by calculating your true ACOS.

I believe showing ebook ads on paperback books (which Amazon will do every minute of the day if you give them the chance) is one of the main reasons ads fail to be profitable. It's also one of the main reasons for fluctuation of ad performance.

With normal targeting, you have no control over whether your ad is showing on a paperback or ebook edition of your target, but Amazon does.

No doubt they divide things to give you a portion of both, but that ratio is probably always changing in accordance to your ad's performance. Better performing ads are likely to get more ebook exposure – they want to keep Kindle Store customers happy by showing them what they're more inclined to buy.

The exposure ratio is also going to be impacted by ad volume. For instance, at busy times of the year such as the lead up to Christmas when there's much more advertising going on, Amazon probably shunt more and more ads over onto paperbacks. Those ads have to go somewhere, even if they're less effective.

4. Does Amazon Use a Relevance Score?

Here's a thought. Facebook ads have a relevance score. They even tell you what it is, and break it down into granular metrics (quality ranking, engagement rate ranking and conversion rate ranking). Google ads have a relevance score as well. They call it a quality score. Likewise, they tell you what it is.

In both cases, the worse your relevance score the less those PPC platforms show your ad. They do this to provide a better experience for their customers. The better your score, the more they show your ad and the *cheaper* they make it to deliver the ad. For instance, the cost per click on Google for a highly relevant ad can be discounted as much as 50%.

On both platforms, bid price and relevance score are used in conjunction to determine ad placement. It's not possible to *bid* your way to the top.

Amazon has never said they have a relevance score. Are they incompetent? Do they fail to meet industry best practice? Do they care less about their customers than the other major platforms?

All these things are possible. But the evidence suggests it's none of them. Amazon is at least as competent as the others, and care as much (if not more) about their customers.

What is it then? Is it just secrecy? It probably is. Amazon is renowned for secrecy. They're a black box. They tell nobody anything. And probably for good reason. The difference between them and the others is that

Amazon is a retail store. Thousands of buy/sell transactions occur every minute, and that attracts scammers. They follow the money. Each tiny bit of information Amazon lets slip about how they operate (including their PPC platform) is an opportunity for scammers to figure out ways to scam better.

But Amazon, while not broadcasting they use a relevancy score as such, do have things to say about the subject. This is from their help pages.

The less relevant or related your book is to your targeting, the less likely it is your ad will perform. Make sure your targeting is relevant to your title, because once the auction market has enough competition, better-performing ads will push out less relevant ones. The more customers click on an ad, the more relevant it becomes.

If your Amazon guru of choice isn't preaching relevance to you, think about getting a new one. They're trying to teach you Salute the Sun, but they don't even know how to do downward dog. Not that it stops them from taking your hard-earned cash.

I don't mean me. I mean for you to be your own guru. All through this series, I've been showing you how standard practice isn't good enough and that sometimes "experts" are clueless. Or worse, clueless but still hoovering up your cash via expensive courses and the like, often with a free funnel to get you in the lop first. The remedy to this is to be your *own* guru. Research. Verify. Test. Treat Google as your friend, and it'll enable you to dig deeper until you find the truth. Then network with people doing the same and share your knowledge.

For all that Amazon don't make a big deal about it, they have a relevance score like Facebook and Google. Their statement even shows that CTR appears to be the main factor in determining the score, but they don't say it's the only one. More on that shortly.

All this adds so much more weight to the need to target ads accurately instead of throwing everything at the wall and seeing what sticks. It explains why ads get shut down. It also shows that bid is not the only important factor to ad placement. The more relevant, the lower you can bid for good ad placement. The less relevant, the higher you have to bid for the same spot. If you can get there at all.

We now know that relevance is critical to success at Amazon ads. And we know that CTR is a major component of how it's calculated. But what, if any, are the other factors?

Conversion rate is a likely candidate. Afterall, nothing says relevance like an actual sale. But CTR is probably more important. It's only an indicator of relevance, rather than the dead-set certainty that a conversion is. But clicks happen a lot more frequently than conversions. Because of their greater number, they're more statistically relevant.

What else might go into the calculation?

It's speculated, among Amazon sellers (of non-book products) that metadata is taken into account. That is, ad copy, search term keywords entered on uploading the product and the product description.

All this is possible. For this reason, it's not a bad idea to use keywords in ad copy especially. If your book is a medical thriller, working that into the ad copy might do some good. The same for your blurb. It may help show that your book is relevant to the big-time medical thriller you're trying to show your ad on.

Despite the theories, I'm not fully convinced. If the metadata does have an influence on the relevance score, it's weighted far less than CTR and conversions.

I'll say this though. If you try to work keywords into your ad copy, do it well. The potential gain from this is far less than the potential loss if your copy stinks. Good copy will drive up the CTR, which is key. Bad copy will reduce it.

For what it's worth, I've trialed keywords in ad copy, and I never noticed a difference in ad placement or cost per click. But I'm not a data guy.

Do your own experiments and see what happens. What I did notice was that my CTR went down. Keywords work great in BookBub ads, but they didn't work well for me on Amazon. Customer expectation and behavior can be different on different platforms.

Since I originally wrote this, it's been confirmed in a webinar with Janet Margot, who set up the ads for books platform on Amazon, that ad copy is not used by Amazon as an indicator of relevance.

It's also contended that reviews play a role in all this. I suspect that concept will be new to most of you. There's so much about Amazon ads that rarely, or never, gets discussed in author circles.

But if reviews are factored in, they're weighted much lower than CTR and conversions. Also, you have no real control over them, or the keyword terms reviewers use when they talk about your books. Be wary of trying to get that control because that's the sort of thing that could trigger Amazon to terminate your account.

It's the same for the keywords you enter on publishing the book. Follow the rules set out for them. Pick the keywords that are best for your book in terms of getting into the right categories and showing up on customer searches. It *is* known, again thanks to Janet, that these seven keywords are important to establish relevance.

What other conclusions can we draw from the presence of a relevance score on Amazon?

A massive one. *Don't run keywords with a poor CTR.* Kill them with fire. They're toxic, and it's speculated that this poison transfers over on an account level. That is, if you have a history of poor ads and keywords, Amazon gives your *account* a lower relevance score. This part is speculation, to be sure.

All of this leads us very nicely into the next chapter. What *is* a good CTR? And what are the uses of the other metrics?

Warning! Since this book was first published some of the "gurus", who until that time had utterly failed to understand the importance of relevance, now talk about it. But they haven't changed their methods – they still recommend the spaghetti-on-the-wall approach. Their "conversion" to relevance is only superficial so as not to look bad. If in doubt here, forget what they say and look at what they do. If their system is all about creating masses of ads, they don't understand how critical relevance is.

5. Expert Use of Ad Metrics

We've already touched on some of the metrics and their uses, but now is the time for a proper introduction.

Impression volume

We've met impression volume, and its importance in previous chapters. Better yet, we've explored the importance of getting *quality* impressions. Because it's quality impressions from good targeting that leads to good clicks.

In PPC marketing, as in so much else of this writing business, nothing stands in isolation. Things all work together toward a unified purpose. At least, when they're working well.

Source your impressions wisely. This is the same thing as saying to target wisely. But still, you want as many as you can get, if they're good. This is the first rudimentary step to scaling, which is the Mount Everest of Amazon ads that's very, very hard to climb.

By its definition, targeting means selecting carefully. This reduces impression volume, but improves its quality. When you cut out the spaghetti-on-the-wall method to see what sticks, you then need to embrace another concept.

A specific book or a general search term (for example, Highland Romance) only gets so many impressions a day. That's it. The supply of customers looking at that product or term is finite. But it's a lot more finite for some than for others.

If a book has a sales rank of 600,000, it's only getting a handful of views a day. Your ad on it will get even less. Therefore, you need to target thousands and thousands of such books to get enough impressions to even be a chance of converting on anything like a regular basis. Essentially, you're wasting your time targeting a low-visibility book like that. The only benefit is that a click, if and when you get it, is cheap.

What you want instead is to target not just highly relevant books, but books with a great sales rank. Anything below 50,000 is the place to start, but better if it's 5,000 or less.

Clicks here will be more expensive. But if you're relevant, they'll be less so. And the more you prove relevance by CTR and conversions off that keyword, the better. This takes us back to the concept of seeding that we discussed earlier.

Relevance lowers your cost per click. Avoiding wasting money on non-targeted keywords allows your bid amount to be higher. Having a higher conversion rate enables you to bid higher too. Combined, these forces enable you to better position yourself to meet the higher costs of showing up on these high-visibility books.

And it's *worth* being on these high-visibility books. Let's do a little bit of basic math.

If a book has a sales rank of 3,000 it's selling about 40 books per day. But how many people are viewing it?

This is an assumption, but the logic is sound. A book that's selling well probably has a fairly good conversion rate. For ads, this is 1 in 10. It would be something similar for organic conversions. On that basis, 40 sales needs about 400 clicks.

If your ad is on that page, at least in the first row of the top Sponsored Product carousel (or it's a Product Display ad) that gives you 400 impressions. Keep in mind that the targeted book is getting clicks, and you're only getting impressions.

Out of 400 impressions, you might average about 1 click a day. (Because you're targeting well, you'll do much better than the standard 1 click to 1,000 impressions). On average, you'll get a conversion about every 10 days.

It doesn't seem like much. But go back to that book with a rank of 600,000 and do the same math. (It's getting a conversion about once a month.) And then halve your conversion rate if it's poorly targeted. That's assuming you even get conversions with poor targeting. This shows you how big the difference between the two approaches is.

Back to our example of 1 sale about every 10 days. Keep in mind, this is just one keyword. If you have 10 such keywords, you're averaging a sale a day.

1 sale every day is enough to tickle Amazon's recommendation engine. It'll start to bring you organic sales.

If you have a hundred such keywords ... well, you can do the math. And it's a lot easier to find 100 good keywords that have high sales rank than tens of thousands of non-targeted keywords with poor sales rank.

Impressions *matter*. They matter big time, because you can't achieve much without them. Just be sure to source them well.

There's a parking break to all this though, which is why scaling is so hard. I'll tackle that in the chapter on scaling.

Click-through rate

Again, we've covered this in detail earlier, so this will be brief. The benefits of a high CTR are many. First, it tells Amazon that your ad resonates with customers. This gives them reason to push it rather than stifle it. Clicks indicate customer interest. We can't know how many clicks derive from the adaptive unconscious situation (expectation clicks) and how many derive from conscious and critical analysis of the ad. But whatever that mix is, they each have baselines and a relevant ad is *always* going to get a higher rate of clicks.

You won't get a surer indication of what customers think of your ad than the CTR. If you're getting a low CTR, then something is wrong with your ad (targeting, cover, title, price and to a lesser extent reviews). This is great news! It enables you to start to pinpoint what's wrong. If you get a great CTR on some targets but not others, your targeting needs improvement. If you get a bad CTR everywhere, it pinpoints that something is wrong with cover, title or price.

A high CTR will also likely mean a lower cost per click because Amazon will favor that ad or keyword. This means you can bid higher.

So, what is a benchmark for a good CTR? For Amazon ads on non-book products the average is 0.36%, or about 1 click for every 279 impressions. Anything below 0.3% or about 1 click per 330 impressions is considered bad. Anything above 0.5% or about 1 click every 200 impressions is considered good.

Google those statistics. Verify. Those are the benchmarks for Amazon ads in general, and it matches my own experience of book ads. It also matches the experience of highly successful authors I know.

Some ads, such as Sponsored Brand and Lockscreen, can have better than average CTR. We'll get to them.

Don't forget the drawback of a bad CTR. Amazon will deem your ad or keyword to be less relevant. This will translate into a higher cost per click and less favorable ad placement.

All of this is why real PPC gurus use and highly value CTR as part of their optimization decisions. But, as we will see, you always make decisions on the basis of all the important metrics considered as a whole rather than just one by itself.

One last thing to note. CTR isn't static. It might decrease over time as your book has been displayed again and again to prospects. Likewise, a boxed set at 99 cents can expect better results than, say, book one of a series that's priced at $3.99 and with no other books in the series yet released.

Cost per click

This is rather self-explanatory, but it's worth noting a few things.

Your CPC is generally lower than your bid. Sometimes as much as 30% lower, sometimes as little as 1% lower. This is a valuable buffer. Generally, it means you can bid higher than you think.

But the relationship between bid and actual CPC is flexible. At times, there might be a large gap. At other times, that gap narrows dramatically.

Is this information useful?

You bet.

When the gap narrows, it's an indicator that competition for that keyword at that bid amount is fierce. This means that you're likely losing a lot of auctions for better ad placement. Or, if you prefer, that you're underbidding.

This is a great trigger to tell you to analyze the keyword's performance. We'll go into this in the optimization chapter, but if the keyword is performing well (keeping in mind whatever overarching strategy you're using for your advertising) raise the bid and watch for increased impressions.

This helps you scale.

Conversion rate

Conversion rate, more commonly known as CVR in PPC marketing circles, is a critical metric.

It may not have escaped you that I said PPC marketing circles. I did *not* say PPC author circles. More on the difference, and why it's important, later.

Conversion rate, simply put, is how many clicks it takes on average to get a sale.

There's no such thing as a good or bad conversion rate. Not on its own. You can only measure CVR against the advertising strategy that you've adopted. The same CVR might be bad if you're aiming for small-scale profit but brilliant if you're aiming for breaking even at a high scale.

So, always keep your strategy in mind when evaluating results. And always keep in mind that when people share ideas on an internet forum of what a good or bad CVR (or any metric) is, they may be basing that on a different strategy from what you're using.

In fact, this is a warning sign. If someone lays down specific benchmark figures about what good CTR and CVR *must* be, it's quite possible that they don't even realize there are different strategies. This places a big question mark over the depth of their knowledge of PPC in general.

But there are benchmarks that you can use as indicators. Especially when you filter those figures through your own chosen strategy. For instance, it's relevant that the average conversion rate across all products on Amazon via PPC advertising is 10%.

As with CTR, I've found this to be spot on for books too.

To put Amazon's 10% CVR into perspective, the average for ecommerce in general is 1.33%.

That's an astounding difference.

Why do Amazon customers convert so much better?

Because Amazon customers have buying intent for the products they're looking at. This is a key difference to other PPC platforms such as Facebook and Google. It ties in, as you would expect, with the earlier comments in this book about targeting. Targeting is critical to success, and it will make or break you as a PPC advertiser.

CVR has value over and above whether or not it's playing its part in helping you meet your advertising strategy.

I don't think I've *ever* seen a keyword that has a low CTR and a high CVR. This is because a low CTR is a predictor of a poor keyword. But I have seen keywords with a high CTR that *didn't* convert.

This is a gold-standard learning opportunity when it happens. So long as you figure out why.

A high CTR indicates your ad is working well. It's generating high interest. The cover, blurb-snippet, reviews and price are doing their job.

So the problem is in one of two places. Poor targeting, or expectations generated by the ad are not being met when the prospect reaches the product page.

By poor targeting, I don't mean the spaghetti-on-the-wall approach this time. I mean that your targeting is fairly close, but not close *enough*. For instance, you might be targeting an epic fantasy book with a coming of age hero. Your book may be epic fantasy with a coming of age hero. People click your ad, but they find your book is noblebright while the book they came from was grimdark.

Sometimes the difference is not as obvious as this. Sometimes you can't even tell what the difference is. Don't give up. Keep looking and you'll spot it. This is the *best* way to learn your subgenre and the micro-niches within it.

This is where most advertisers fail. They don't do the work to figure out what went wrong. They may switch off a keyword because it's not working for them, only to start up a new keyword with the same mistake the next day. If you're doing PPC advertising, you *will* make mistakes. Those who succeed at PPC advertising learn from their mistakes. Those who fail keep repeating them.

Do the work. I can't say it simpler than that.

The other reason for a high CTR but a low CVR is that something is wrong with the product. Maybe the blurb is bad. Or your preview. Or you have bad reviews. Whatever the case, dig deep and find the answers.

If you have a high CVR off some keywords, but not others, it indicates a targeting issue. If you have a low CVR off all keywords, it indicates a product issue.

One last point. Just as with CTR, but even more so, conversions are influenced by price. For example a boxed set at 99 cents might convert as high as 1 in 5. Book 1 of a series at full price without the follow up books will often struggle to do 1 in 10.

Sales

This is the most self-explanatory metric of all. Except it isn't. Not quite.

The sales figure on the Amazon ad dashboard gives the full price of the book or books sold. But you as the author only get 70% of this depending on your royalty tier. Books priced below $2.99 or above $9.99 only pay 35% royalties, but the sale amount in the Amazon dashboard is always the full sale price.

When looking at this metric, be sure to convert the "sales" into actual dollars earned according to your royalty rate.

Also, paperback sales show in here as well, if you're advertising a paperback. This massively skews your figures. Paperbacks sell for roughly three times the price, but you only earn a similar amount in royalties as you do from an ebook. Be wary of this, grasshopper. It can make a shocker of an ad seem like Cinderella dressed for the ball.

One more thing. While I don't buy into the concept that Amazon reporting is inaccurate, *at all*, it is delayed. All those hundreds of millions of clicks take time to sort out. The attribution window is 14 days. But most sales and page reads will show within a few days. Just don't expect data to show immediately. Allow for a spread.

ACOS

This metric is much maligned. But somewhat unfairly. It does work well for some people, in some specific situations. As always, there's never a one-size-fits-all answer, and bear that in mind when discussions of ACOS crop up online.

All that being said, the majority of indie authors are in KU, and ACOS doesn't account for page-read income. This alone renders ACOS completely inaccurate (for authors in KU).

Likewise, ACOS doesn't account for sell through to other books in the series. Again, this renders it completely inaccurate (unless you have no other books in the series).

Long story short, most folks are better off ignoring ACOS.

6. How to Measure Ad Results

I've made a choice at this point. This is a book of advanced strategies, so I'm not going to go down the rabbit warren of math for all the different ways of calculating the results of ads. It would take too long. Nor is it necessary.

What's important here is that you have an overview of the different methods, including their advantages and disadvantages. From that, you can make your own choice on how best to proceed. Whichever method you choose, the method of calculation is easy enough to figure out and also readily available from other sources.

But I do have to touch on the math briefly in a few places. And the terminology used in author circles.

Most authors would say that measuring ad results is about determining the ROI. That is, the return on investment. ROI is a popular metric in business and finance, but it's a *strategic* assessment. It's usually used to analyze a situation as a whole. For instance, the calculation of ROI on selling an investment home will account for all the expenses involved in acquiring it in the first place, maintaining it and finally selling it. We're talking purchase price, legal fees, bank fees and mortgage interest and maintenance costs etc. On selling, the profit includes rent and sale price.

The formula for ROI is:

Net profit / total investment x 100

Note, because ROI is a strategic view of things, the formula uses *net* profit and *total* investment. In indie publishing, you should really use the formula to calculate something like how financially successful a book was. Net profits would be royalties and the payout for page reads. Total investment would be the price of covers, editing and marketing.

So, ROI is really the wrong term to look at how successful *one* component of an overall investment strategy is. What we want to do with Amazon ads is measure how effective the ads themselves are, not what overall return the book makes.

As it happens, when we expand our horizon away from author circles, we find that the marketing world was there long before us. Big surprise, huh?

Please allow me to introduce you to ROAS, aka return on ad spend.

Now we're talking. This is what we want. The correct term with the correct formula for what we want to do – pin down ad results.

This is the ROAS formula:

$$\textit{Ad revenue} - \textit{ad cost} / \textit{ad cost} \times 100$$

In concept, it's very similar to ROI. But ROAS is granular. ROI lumps everything together. ROAS sheets profit or loss directly home to individual ads or keywords. It pinpoints with great focus. It calculates *ad* returns, not returns influenced by other sales drivers like covers, blurbs, new releases and the recommendation engine.

But that's my preference. Choose what you believe is the best way forward. I use ROAS because it's the professional term for measuring ad performance, and also because it reinforces that when judging ads, they should be viewed on their merits alone and not other factors.

But things are always more complicated than they seem. ROAS is usually calculated as a ratio. For instance, 1:2, which means for every $1.00 spent on ads, $2.00 was returned. But it's also sometimes expressed as a percentage, which is what I prefer. It can also be calculated two different ways. One way will use net ad revenue (ad revenue – ad cost) and the other gross ad revenue.

I prefer the first way. The second is more common. It doesn't really matter which method you choose, so long as you know which is which and compare like to like.

Indie authors also use the ROI formula in different ways to calculate ad return. Some use ad data only and not the strategic data ROI is intended for. That's okay. It comes to the same thing. Then again, some gurus advise a mixed approach, and use *all* profits in the formula but only *selected* expenses. I'm *not* okay with this.

Confused yet?

You can use whichever formula you want, and call it whatever you want. What counts is the data you calculate with. Do you restrict it to ad data? Good. This is tactical rather than strategic. Do you use all data to determine the overall book ROI? Cool. This is strategic. This is what ROI is for. Do you use all profits but only some expenses? Not cool, grasshopper. This is putting bubbles in grape juice and calling it champagne.

Hopefully, all this will become clear as we dive into the various methods in use for measuring ad results.

The comparison method

This method works with totals. It compares total ad spend against total book profit. As long as your profit outmatches your ad spend, you're, well, winning! Something like that.

The benefit of this approach is simplicity. It's pretty easy to do. As long as you're making a profit, things are okay. And the bigger the profit, the better. The disadvantage is that it's wildly inaccurate as a measure of how your ads are working.

Earlier, I mentioned ads can have a direct influence on conversions and an indirect influence. The indirect influence is the recommendation engine and organic sales.

The comparison method takes every single conversion you ever get and attributes them directly to your ads.

This really is turning grape juice into champagne. Or trying to.

Even if you start from ground zero with no conversions at all, and then begin to advertise and get sales, the method is still inaccurate. Give a well-packaged book some visibility, and it starts to sell itself.

If you're already selling, the method is hopeless.

Either way, how do you determine which ads are working and which aren't? What are your benchmarks for success? How do you measure if one ad is hitting them and another isn't? How do you know if your ads are generating a negative return, but it's being masked by organic sales?

Any adviser who preaches the comparison method should issue it with a disclaimer. Warning! This method will make me look like a genius because it'll attribute every sale you *ever* make to the ad tactics I've taught you.

Damn. Makes me wish I'd thought of it myself. If people thought I was a genius and my methods so wonderfully effective, I'd sell more books…

Baseline comparison

This is similar to the above, but establishes a weekly, monthly or longer baseline first. The baseline is the average number of books converted for the title being advertised.

Once you commence advertising, you calculate ad effectiveness exactly as in the previous method, only you measure revenue generated over and above the baseline instead of assuming all profit stems from advertising.

The benefit of this approach is that it's still pretty easy. It's also much more realistic than the first method.

On the downside? You do need a baseline first. So, obviously, it's not much good for launches.

More importantly, there's no such thing as an accurate baseline of conversions. Month by month, even week by week, sales slide. New releases or promotion of a backlist book can raise it though. Catching onto an also-bought can raise it, and falling off an also-bought can lower it. Time of year influences the baseline too.

It also suffers from the same defect as the first. It still lumps some organic sales together with ad-generated sales. There's some sort of argument to be made for this, but not much. As time goes by, the argument gets weaker and weaker. At the risk of repeating myself, books can sell by themselves. Ads might start the ball rolling, but they don't play tennis. For tennis, you need a court, net, players and racquets. Advertising might be the ball, but the rest is organic sales.

As you can see, I'm not a fanboy of this method either. But it's a lot better than the first.

Direct attribution

This is the standard approach. It relies on the Ad Dashboard. The sales come in on ads and keywords, and you measure ad or keyword performance with the ROAS formula.

Detractors of the method say that Amazon gets it all wrong and that sales are inaccurately reported.

It's certainly true that reporting is delayed, sometimes up to 14 days. If you use this method, take that into account. Give an ad or keyword time to start showing results.

For myself, I don't believe the hullabaloo about Amazon reporting. Nor do I believe the conspiracy theories that Amazon defrauds authors. There's a lot of hatred out there for Amazon. Big business tends to generate that. And it's directly in the interest of a person selling books or courses to preach the comparison method. It's a lot harder for their teachings to fail when *all* profit is attributed to them.

The real problem was that Amazon didn't report on clicks that generated page reads. That *was* a serious problem. Note that I've used past tense here. Amazon have updated their metrics and now report page reads triggered by ad clicks.

Hallelujah!

Even before this though, it was easy enough to establish a ratio of sales to page reads. As discussed previously, for many people this is currently 1:2.

Work out what yours is. It's a good thing to know, and it's not hard. Not at all. When you have it, keep an eye on it from time to time. KU is growing. The ratio will change over time.

Sales and page reads go up or down depending on the sales rank of the book. They fluctuate a lot. But the ratio between them? So long as the price of the book remains steady, the ratio remains fairly steady.

For those of you who use Advantage ad accounts, Amazon still doesn't give the ad generated page reads, so I've retained the workaround in this update of the book.

This is how it goes. Once you have your ratio, then you can add the estimated page-read payout to the sales figure from the Ad Dashboard.

Using the ROAS formula given above, ad revenue is made up of recorded sales and estimated page reads. Or, if you have a regular account that does report page reads, ad revenue is made up of recorded sales and recorded page reads.

This is all pretty simple. It's the best method so far. By a long way, in my view.

It's true that the influence of advertising in causing indirect sales isn't recorded. I'm okay with that. I'm not trying to calculate overall profit here. I'm trying to establish ad and keyword performance so that I know which ones are working and which ones aren't. This allows me to direct more budget to the good ones and turn off the bad ones.

If you really wanted to, you could estimate what the indirect sales are. This is very hard to do though. I'd suggest, at a minimum, it's 10%. It's probably more. But the more ad conversions you have, the higher it will be. At lower levels, you're only tickling the interest of the recommendation engine. At higher levels, the effect snowballs.

If you know a way to estimate indirect sales with reasonable accuracy, please let me know. I'd love to discuss that.

Direct attribution with flow through

This is the Big Momma of calculating ad effectiveness. It's the boss. And it's been around the block a time or two. It knows what it's doing – so my advice is not to mess with it.

It's the most accurate of all the methods, but also the most time consuming.

But once you've done the figures, you've done them. It's not really very hard at all.

What are the figures? The same as the previous method. Only this time you add estimated sell through and estimated read through rates for *subsequent* books to the ad revenue component of the ROAS formula.

That's it. It's the one measure of ad effectiveness to rule them all.

But that's just my opinion. Tread your own path, grasshopper.

7. Why Ads Die

It's sometimes said that ads die. This is just the way it is. What you have to do is keep creating ads to stay ahead of the game.

This stems from a complete lack of understanding of how PPC advertising platforms work. If your ads die, there's a *reason*. Find it and fix it. That's the path to success.

PPC advertising is a feedback loop. You put something out there, and get results back that you learn from. Then you refine. Keep doing this. Giving up and starting from scratch again is dooming yourself to repeating the same mistakes.

Another way of saying this is that ads don't die. Amazon kills them. They kill them because they're not providing a good customer experience.

If you're on the wrong side of this, it feels bad. I know. I've been there. But once you understand and accept it, it's the path to victory.

Knowledge is power. It's an advantage over your competitors. Dig deep to find that knowledge, and question standard practice. Underneath lies *best* practice.

Amazon likes to give things a fair go. They'll trial an ad to see if it's working. The better it resonates, the more they'll show it. But after that initial burst, if it doesn't resonate, they'll stifle it quickly. Probably by shifting it to poorer ad placement such as on paperbacks, farther back along the carousel or on the bottom Sponsored Product carousel that sometimes shows just above the reviews. They don't wait for statistical perfection to do this. They act quickly.

This turns an already poor ad into a leper.

There are other reasons an ad can start well and then taper off. For instance, the target keywords can relate to books that are falling in rank. They may be tailing off after a BookBub or something like that. When their visibility drops, so too does visibility of your ad.

The other reason is that you've tapped out the target audience. They've already read the book, and you struggle to find new readers at the same rate that you did when the book was new.

This can happen. It really can. When it does, it's a gradual decline in CTR and CVR. But you have to sell a lot of books to worry about this.

8. How to Interpret Amazon's Suggested Bids

I said in book one of this series that Amazon's suggested bids are generally the starting point of where to bid, if you can afford to do so. This is not what many people think. But then again, it depends on who you ask. There are very successful advertisers out there bidding two, three and even *four* times the suggested bid – as a matter of routine.

And profiting.

It's all a matter of perspective and strategy. And the situation you're in. More than anything, it's about the situation that you can work *toward* putting yourself in.

Let's explore the suggested bid issue.

You can bid 25 cents when the suggested bid is 70 cents, which is often recommended. And when you get very few impressions, then you can up your bid by 2 cent increments. Again, this is often recommended.

My appraisal of that tactic in book one was that it was the long, slow, boring way to advertising death.

My opinion hasn't changed.

Amazon sets that suggested bid by using the data of what other people are successfully bidding for that keyword with ads similar to yours. It's hard to know exactly what they mean when they say this. I take it to mean the ads in question have a similar relevance score to yours.

If you choose, you can believe that Amazon are trying to rip you off. They suggest a bid way, way higher than necessary to steal money from you.

But the proof is in the pudding. Bid low, and see how few impressions you get. Bid higher, and watch those impressions increase. It's as simple as that. Amazon isn't fixing the race. It *is* a race. You're competing against many, many other authors. The higher bids win. The lower bids lose. That's not Amazon rigging the system. That's reality.

You may not like that reality. Who does? But failing to accept it is a surefire way to ensure you will never succeed at Amazon ads.

Look at this in the perspective of the strategies detailed in the beginning of this book. Several years ago, most authors were on the small-scale profit model. Competition was lower. In fact, it was *much* lower. This is why some early adopters of Amazon advertising were able to do well.

But some of those same authors don't advertise now. They got lucky early on, but their skill and knowledge weren't enough to keep up with a maturing PPC platform.

That's a critical factor. The platform has matured. Competition is now fierce. Many, many authors now have the long series' and boxed sets and high conversion rates that enable them to move up through the strategies.

This is what has lifted Amazon's suggested bids. Competition. Not Amazon.

If you use strategies from several years ago, you're not going to be able to compete. The only answer to this is to work toward putting yourself in a competitive position, or to make the most of the small-scale profit model. But by necessity, it will be very small scale and it won't turn over enough sales to stimulate the recommendation engine.

The truth is that you probably should start bidding a few cents *above* the suggested bid price in your experimentation phase. This gets you in front of the masses who go with what Amazon suggests. Likewise, always avoid bidding with "standard" numbers. For instance, bid at 71 cents instead of 70. Or 86 cents instead of 85. This tends to get you above the masses too.

Still not buying the higher-bid approach? I don't blame you. A lot of people have been taught the low-bid myth, and what I'm saying is difficult to accept. But if you're following the low-bid advice, are you getting lots of impressions? Are you getting clicks off those impressions? Do those clicks convert? Have you scaled up? Are you getting enough sales to stimulate the recommendation engine?

It's nearly impossible to do any of those things with a low-bid strategy.

You may have read all this and dismissed it. As I said in book one, all I ask is that if you *have* to bid low to bid affordably, please don't frame your philosophy around that fact permanently. Many of your competition won't. They'll take the steps needed to ensure they can bid higher.

Are you able to do the same?

Let's tackle the issue of Amazon's suggested bids by comparing it to all other aspects of their business model.

Everything Amazon does is about trying to lower prices. They're the pinup model for low prices and high volume. It doesn't matter if it's books, wine glasses, socks or pasta sauce.

Selling ad space to authors is just another product to them. They want a high-volume uptake of the service. In the end, they'll make more money this way. It's in their interest to keep bids and subsequent CPC as low as possible to encourage the highest possible usage by authors. What's raising bids is not Amazon but author competition.

The suggested bids are actually conservative. Many authors bid far higher. They just don't talk about it for fear of getting shot down by the hive mind that prefers lower bids.

But the hive mind can be called something else. Mediocrity. Most people don't sell well. Most people don't know how to crack indie publishing. Most people are following out-of-date advice from gurus who don't actually sell books. Success requires a can-do attitude of questioning standard practice and rising above the hive mind.

If you dare.

Bidding lower is still possible. You may even be able to make a profit. But, generally, you're not going to get enough impression volume to turn on the tap. You'll pick up a few conversions here and there, but you'll never be able to scale and trigger the recommendation engine.

When looking at the suggested bid price and determining your own bid, first determine which of the main strategies you're following.

Also, keep in mind that the bid is not the CPC. CPC sometimes runs 20% to 30% lower. But not always. You have to keep a very sharp eye on this. And, as I've pointed out earlier, remember that the bid is just one of the factors that Amazon use to determine who wins the ad auction. Bidding high on a keyword with low relevance is generally not a good idea. Better to bid high on a relevant target, and decrease costs with a high CVR.

But at the end of the day, you can only bid as high as the sales and page reads, combined with CVR, sell through and read-through rate allow. Those are the true limiting factors and not the bid.

That's looking at the glass half empty. Looking at it with the glass half full, sales and page reads, combined with CVR, sell through and read-through rate are the growth factors, *all within your control*, that will allow you to determine your Amazon advertising strategy.

If you get anything from this chapter, don't let it be that low bids are bad. Or that high bids are good. Neither is the point.

The point is that what you can afford to bid is under your control. What you write, and how you package it are choices you make.

You are in control. Not Amazon. Not competing authors. Not the hive mind. You.

9. Profit Versus Perfect Data

The aim of marketing, and the purpose of ads, no matter your strategy or tactics, is to make a profit. Either in the short term or the long term.

And ads work. Especially Amazon ads. They serve on a platform where prospects are engaged and primed to buy.

All that is required is to understand how that platform operates and gain mastery of it.

I say all that is required, but I also know it's *hard*.

Correct knowledge to guide you, and hard work will overcome this. Myths will hold you back.

The greatest myth of all is that you can't optimize your keywords because even a long serving one doesn't generate enough data to be statistically relevant.

On this basis, some people suggest you need to forget about optimizing keywords, and that you should bid low, target wide and basically hope for the best. And when your ads die, start new ones. Proponents of this philosophy also say a click is a click is a click.

This is not how I manage my PPC advertising. I've never met another professional PPC advertiser, who has managed to scale, operate that way either. Nor have I ever seen that attitude in non-author PPC circles.

You *can* optimize keywords. It *is* possible. And it's the pathway to success.

Before we go on, what's considered statistically relevant data?

I'm not going to go into the math. I'm not qualified to go into the math. But essentially, statistical relevance is having enough data so that you can say an event is *not* caused by chance. Or at least, that you can be 95% confident that the result was not caused by chance.

Variance plays a role in this too.

Flip a coin. You'll get either heads or tails. You have an equal chance of getting either.

Flip that coin three times. You might get three heads in a row. Or none. That's variance.

But keep flipping the coin. You might flip a hundred heads in a row. It's possible. But it's not likely. Variance can turn a simple event into an extreme.

How many clicks do you need for statistical relevance when selling books? Your conversion rate has a big influence over that. But I've seen estimates ranging from hundreds of clicks to a thousand.

You're not likely to get that many clicks on a keyword.

This is why the data analysts give up on optimization.

But this is why marketers succeeded at PPC advertising. They don't care about seeking perfect data. Perfect data has nothing to do with making a profit. It's the enemy of profit. It's paralysis by analysis.

Let's go back to flipping that coin.

You might flip 100 heads in a row. But you probably won't. You have a 50% chance of getting heads and a 50% chance of getting tails, and over time you'll get about as many of one as the other.

Google "probability distribution bell curve". This gives you a visual representation.

Variance means you can get extreme results. But probability distribution clusters things back up.

If you're tossing coins, you can be confident of getting heads pretty soon. Or tails. Variance is the chance that things might stretch out.

We're not interested in variance. We're interested in probability distribution. We're not interested in perfect data. We're interested in making a profit.

Selling a book is not flipping a coin. You might convert at 1 in 10 clicks. This makes it harder.

But from 10 clicks, you still have a good chance of converting before you reach 10. (A 49.9% chance I believe). If you wait until 20 clicks, your chances are much better.

Of course, because of variance, you *might* go 100 or 1,000 clicks on that keyword before you get a conversion. (I could win the Nobel Peace Prize too. But probably not.)

This is the critical thing though. You'll have more than one keyword.

Say you have a hundred. Or five hundred. Are they all going to get struck down by the dreaded variance disease?

No.

Half of those keywords will convert *before* the 10 clicks. Many more will convert before 20 clicks.

What does this mean? You have a bunch of highly targeted keywords that *should* work for you. A conversion on such a keyword is proving it. A second is proving it more.

These are the keywords you keep. At least, if they're converting at a CPC that's meeting your strategy.

The non-converting keywords are the ones you turn off.

Will that turn off some keywords that could have ended up being good if you waited for perfect data?

Yes.

I can sleep at night doing that. I don't need to bleed money to discover which ones they are. But note, while you may kill off a few of those, you're also killing the duds.

Save your resources of time and money for keywords that are proven to perform. Don't chase perfect data on which to base decisions.

But exactly when do you have *enough* data to turn off a keyword?

Once again, marketing has been here before authors and they have a formula. Two, in fact.

Both formulas are based on the known (preferable) or expected (acceptable) conversion rate.

This is the first. It's considered to have a moderate probability of accuracy:

100 / conversion rate % = clicks to wait

Here's an example:

100 / 10 = 10 clicks to wait

This is the second. It's considered to have a higher probability of accuracy:

100 / conversion rate % x 2 = clicks to wait

Here's an example:

100 / 10 x 2 = 20 clicks to wait

To put things into an everyday perspective with something we're familiar with, here's the second formula as it relates to a coin toss:

100 / 50 x 2 = 4 coin tosses to wait

With 4 tosses, I'd be pretty confident of getting heads at least once. What about you?

There's another way to look at this. It might help you picture things a bit more strategically. Imagine you live in the desert. You've planted a long row of maize. Five hundred kernels to be exact.

You've tilled and fertilized the soil. You've planted the maize. And you've watered it all in to get things going.

Ten days later, you have 250 nice little maize plants reaching for the sun. You also have 250 empty spaces.

No problem. Not all maize germinates at the same time. In fact, not every kernel germinates no matter how long you wait. Not all kernels are viable.

Now, you have a choice. You live in the desert, remember. Water is a finite resource. It's downright scarce.

Do you water only the maize that has germinated? Or do you water the entire row, germinated and non-germinated alike?

Let's say you keep watering it all. Over the next few days more maize germinates. Say another 50 shoots come up. You've proved a point. Some of those empty spots were viable.

On the other hand. Because you spread that precious resource of water around, the first lot that came up are now wilted and their growth is stunted. The later-germinating ones too. They'll never produce the crop that they could have.

But, if you directed your scarce water supply only to the 250 that came up initially, they're doing well.

In this scenario, the maize kernels are your keywords and the water is your time and money. You only have so much of either to go around. Direct it wisely rather than seeking statistical perfection. Statistical perfection doesn't put food on the table. Profit does.

This is one more reason a high CVR is desirable. It saves you money by requiring less clicks to convert, builds relevancy, and also offers quicker statistical confidence.

At this point, I'm going to say that statistics and probability equations are good, but the art and science of PPC marketing is all about reducing the *randomness* of events.

Flipping a coin and getting heads or tails is entirely random. But PPC marketers don't play fair. They use a weighted coin. Targeting is the first step in this. Random targeting gives random results. The better the targeting, the more confidence you can have that it *is* a good keyword.

Over and above that, CTR is an indicator of success. It's like an in-car navigation system telling you if you're on track (or off track) before you reach your destination.

Keep in mind that it's an indicator, not a guarantee. PPC marketers weigh up all factors before they make a decision. They look at the metrics as a whole. This is called optimization. It's about profit rather than statistical perfection, and it's the subject of the next chapter.

One final word. If you wait for statistical relevance, the keyword you're using may well play out before you reach that point. Books rise in sales rank on release, and then fall. Once it's fallen beyond a certain point, it's no longer capable of generating enough impressions and clicks to be meaningful. There aren't many targets that stay high enough in rank to keep generating clicks on your ad long enough for you to get statistical relevance. But the answer is not to ignore keywords and focus only on overall ad performance. That is sometimes suggested, but not by advertisers actually selling books.

One *last* final word, I promise. It might interest you to know that even the concept of statistical significance as it relates to advertising is questioned in some prestigious circles. If you want to follow up on that, Google "Debunking ad testing."

What do I always say, grasshopper? *Keep digging for the truth.*

10. How Experts Optimize

Optimization is the place where many of the things we've been talking about intersect. It will make or break your success as a PPC advertiser.

But it's complicated. Therefore, this chapter is complicated. In the famous words of Maxwell Smart, sorry about that, Chief.

How does it work?

Optimization is like a seesaw. You may know it as a teeter-totter. If you apply pressure on one end, the other lifts (profit). If you lift one end, the other drops (investing in loss). If you keep the board level, it's, well, level (breaking even).

We looked at the important PPC metrics before, but now we'll revisit them with some different nuances.

Impressions

Impressions are the raw material with which you work to try to shape your vision. You optimize them by targeting like for like.

You need about 1,000 impressions to get an idea of how a keyword is going. But the first true step of optimizing is to see how fast they're coming in.

If they're only coming in at ten or twenty a day, you have a problem. It's going to take forever to get conversions. A lot here hinges on which strategy you're aiming for, but this is slow even for the small-scale profit model. At this rate, it's going to take a couple of months, or more, to reach 1,000 impressions. And you might only get one or two conversions a year.

The question to ask is why is the impression volume so low? Investigate. Does the target keyword have a bad sales rank? If so, it's not capable of generating impressions.

I switch these off. Sometimes. If it's a debut book and it never took off, I kill it. It was a mistake to target it in the first place. If it's a book that used to have good sales rank, but doesn't anymore, what are the prospects that it will again? Is it part of a series? How frequently does the author release? Make a judgement as to whether or not you think the book will attain a good sales rank in the future. If so, there's no harm in keeping the keyword switched on if you've been happy with its performance. This will preserve your relevance to it.

But if the keyword does have sales rank and you're still not getting many impressions, look at your bid. Is it high enough? It probably isn't. If you can afford to, raise the bid. Ultimately, you only get what you pay for.

Also, check for relevance. Amazon may be stifling impressions because they don't think it's giving customers on the other end a good experience. You should have caught this in the targeting phase, but sometimes this sort of thing slips through.

If impressions are flowing in at a reasonable rate, check for your CTR. 1,000 impressions is enough to start to judge this. If it's a good keyword, you might have ten clicks or more. Probably, you can expect two or three. If you have none, recheck your relevance. If you're super-confident it's a good match, wait until maybe 1,500 impressions. If you realize it isn't a good match, switch it off.

The minimum benchmark here is about one click per thousand impressions. But if in doubt, let things go a little longer. I don't think I've ever seen a keyword start off with a low CTR and then shift gears into a higher one, but I guess it's possible. Kill off bad keywords quickly, but give them a chance first.

CTR

A good CTR indicates the ad resonates with the target audience. Compared to conversions, it has a high volume. This makes it more statistically relevant.

You're (generally) looking for a CTR of about 1 in 500. A CTR of 1 in 100 or higher isn't uncommon for really good keywords.

You may have read or heard (in author circles) that 1 in 1,000 is your target. This isn't a target, but an average. It includes all the people running ads who haven't learned how to run them properly.

Success comes from seeking best practice, not accepting standard practice. If you're doing what everyone else is doing, how can you hope to rise to the top?

If your CTR is bad, Amazon penalizes you. CPC goes up, and favorable ad positioning goes down.

I'm willing to keep a few keywords with a CTR of around 1 in 1,000, but not many. And only if they're converting. Generally, this will be a traditionally published author with a high sales rank. I say a high sales rank because this will generate a flow of impressions and conversions. It makes it worthwhile to keep, so long as it's contributing fairly regular conversions.

But if the impression volume is low, and consequentially the conversion volume, I'll turn off an ad with a bad CTR even if it converts occasionally. It's not worth having at the risk of making my ads and campaigns appear less relevant to Amazon.

If your CTR is bad, look toward your targeting to find out why. If you don't think it's this, look toward your book cover, title and blurb snippet. Adjusting these might improve CTR, but this is problematic because of expense and time.

Apart from targeting, price is the main driver of CTR. Lower it, and CTR tends to rise. But all this is a balance. It's no good having a better CTR if your profit plummets.

If your CTR is great, but you're not converting, look toward your product page for answers. And your preview. Such a scenario indicates your cover and ad copy are working, but your blurb, reviews and preview have significant faults. Especially the blurb and preview because the overall review star rating is included in the ad.

It's always worth checking, and then rechecking your targeting though. Bad targets are often easy to spot, and the CTR is bad. The trickiest scenario though is when your targeting is *almost* perfect, but not quite. This leads people to click through with high interest but to get put off on the blurb or preview. Not because it's bad but because it's not quite what they're looking for.

If you do this deliberately, it's called adjacent targeting. It's almost like for like, but not quite. It can work well, or it can fail. You have to test and monitor this. Either way, deliberate or accidental, it's a great learning opportunity to discover the nuances of your niche.

CVR

Conversion rate is the most critical metric of them all. Except, really, it isn't.

I hope you're beginning to see now how all the metrics work together like cogs in a machine toward the same purpose. Small cogs. Big cogs. Slow cogs and fast cogs. *They're all linked.* When one has trouble, they all have trouble.

But what does CVR tell us in isolation?

First, it's confirmation of your targeting. Especially once you have several conversions off a keyword.

You're looking for a CVR of about 10%. That's very, very approximate. You're looking for keywords that have enough impression volume to generate a stream of clicks and a smaller stream of conversions.

Most importantly, CVR isn't telling you much about how your ad is working. It's telling you about how well your blurb, reviews and preview are working. But especially the blurb.

If your CTR is high, the ad is working. If your CVR is high, your book is working.

Clicks

At the risk of repeating myself, to scale at even a small level, you need impression volume. Impression volume offers the possibility of a lot of clicks. Clicks offer an opportunity for conversions.

If you have an ad or keyword that's getting a lot of impressions but few clicks, try to figure out why. It means something. Find out what, and learn. Then, turn it off. It's hurting your relevance score.

But you might be getting a really high CTR, but still the clicks are few and far between. This is an impression volume problem. Is it worth keeping these keywords going?

First, see why the impressions are low. Is it that you're bidding too low? Fix that, if you can. But you can only bid what your book situation (price, page reads, read-through rate etc. allows). Or, is it a ranking issue of the target book? If it's not good it can't generate impressions. But, does that author release regularly or get frequent BookBubs? It might be worth keeping the keyword going because the future rank is likely to spike and rain impressions on you down the track.

If not, I tend to switch these keywords off. They're not bad keywords. They're just not going to get me anywhere soon. And in this business, time is money. Keep advertising as simple and easy as possible so you have more time for writing.

When to kill off a keyword that's getting lots of clicks at a good CTR is a hard decision. It goes back to statistical relevance. Revisit the chapter on profit versus perfect data for my opinions on that. But essentially, don't wait for full statistical relevance. That'll send you broke. Aim for the number of clicks you think it will take on average to get a conversion. Then a little bit more, but not much. Most of all, check your targeting again. If you spot the problem there, you've learned something about your niche. Switch it off. If targeting still seems good, give it that minimum of expected clicks to convert. Wait and see. But not too long.

Bid

Optimizing your bid for a keyword is the most difficult of tasks.

A good place to start is to see where your current bid is landing you. A Sponsored Product carousel may have twenty or more rows in it. If you're using a search term type keyword (such as billionaire bad boy) there will be page after page of search returns. Where are you landing on all this and are you happy with that placement?

Ad placement does matter. It has its own chapter coming up shortly. Suffice to say here, your bid amount is a key element of where your ad is shown. It's not the only element, as we've seen that relevance plays a large role, but it's still critical.

How high you bid impacts ad placement, and this should be considered in conjunction with the advertising strategy you're using.

When deciding bid amount, it's useful to see where any particular bid places you. Find your ad on the keyword, and note exactly where it appears. Obviously, if you run an ad blocker, you'll need to switch it off first.

Then go into your ads dashboard and change the bid. Maybe lift it to $2.00 or lower it to 30 cents. Escape out of the dashboard and see where your ad now shows. Changes are usually instant, but you have to get out of the ads dashboard first.

This lets you see where high bids and low bids place you. You're only doing this for a few minutes, so you're unlikely to get a high-bid click during that time.

This process gives you a good idea of how the bid auction works, what the competition is doing and how much they're paying to show where they show. Keep in mind though, their CPC will be higher or lower according to relevance.

Questions to ask yourself are where do you want your ad to show? And how much can you afford to pay for that?

Setting up a keyword is different from optimizing one with a history of data. When setting one up, base your bid off the factors above and your estimate of the conversion rate.

If you think it will convert 1 in 5 clicks, or 1 in 15 or whatever the case may be, set your bid a bit higher than what that number of clicks would cost to bring you to a break-even point. Or your chosen strategy. Keep in mind that CPC is sometimes significantly lower than the bid, so you can bid a bit higher than you think. Experiment with this. Maybe you can bid 10 cents higher. Or 20 or 30. Find out, otherwise you risk strangling your impression volume with too low a bid. *You want your average CPC to align with your overarching strategy, not your bid.* Many people, including those who charge hundreds of dollars for their advertising courses, miss this opportunity.

What you bid is one of the most powerful tools in adjusting the seesaw. Lift it or lower it according to your strategy. If you're making a profit, great, but maybe you want to increase it to get more impressions and reach break even or invest-in-loss to increase organic sales. Maybe your launch is finished and you want to move from the invest-in-loss strategy to break even.

Bid amount isn't static. Change it as your situation and goal changes. Maybe a keyword converts, but not at profit. Lower the bid a little. See if you stay where you were on the ad placement. Adjust. Monitor. Balance. Be adaptable. This might muddy data analysis, but keep in mind that your end goal is profit, not perfect data expensively acquired.

How do you know if you're making a profit or loss? Strap yourself in. There's a little math ahead.

I introduced you to the ROAS formula earlier. It's the official way to measure ad performance. Here it is again.

$$Ad\ revenue - ad\ cost\ /\ ad\ cost \times 100$$

The "ad revenue" part is more complicated than it seems. It can also be either gross or net. I prefer net. It should also include estimated profits of sell through to subsequent books. Additionally, if you're in KU, it should include profits from page reads and estimated read through.

ROAS is the way to calculate ad performance, but it's also the way to optimize bid amount. These two factors are opposite ends of the seesaw.

Let's run through a real-life example. This is one of the keywords I have running at the moment. The advertised book is a boxed set priced at $7.99 with a KENPC page count (available under the Promote and Advertise tab on the bookshelf) of 828. The keyword is an ASIN.

These are the metrics for the keyword. Bid: $1.21. Impressions: 14,087. Clicks: 94. CTR: 0.67% (1 in 149). Spend: $58.10. CPC: $0.62. Orders: 8. Sales: $63.92. ACOS: 90.89%.

A few observations before we do the calculations. Targeting by ASIN works. These are good metrics, despite a high bid. But that bid (and relevancy) is landing me first on the Sponsored Product carousel, and the actual CPC is much, much less. As for the CVR, Amazon doesn't give us one, but it's one conversion every 11.75 clicks. This doesn't include full page read borrows, so we have to factor that in. This is easy now because Amazon gives us the data. But not for some Advantage accounts. For that reason, I've let my example below of doing it the old way stand.

Looking at my KDP Reports tab, and going to the Month-to-Date tab and sorting by the US store alone (or the UK store if measuring UK ad performance) for the previous month of data, I see the book had 15 sales and 29,468 page reads.

29,468 page reads divided by the page count of 828 gives me 35.5 full page reads. That's a ratio of 1 sale to 2.36 full page reads.

Sales and borrows fluctuate somewhat. So, if possible, I like to dig deeper to get more reliable figures. Because this is an old book, I can do that.

I can go into the Historical tab, select only the US store and the title in question and sort by the last 12 months. I'm only going to look at the last 3 months though, because KU is always growing and I want an up-to-date ratio.

Adding the last three months up (ebook sales only), I have 89 sales. Do the same for page reads, and I have 176,242. That's 212.85 full page reads.

That's a ratio of 1 to 2.39, almost identical to the other calculation. The sales to page read ratio is usually consistent, no matter what some people tell you when they try to talk you into just measuring total ad spend against total profits.

If, for some reason, there *is* a difference, then you could pick the midpoint between the two or just use the lower ratio to be conservative.

I *am* conservative, so in this case I'm going to pick the lower ratio to work with anyway, even though there's barely a difference.

The royalty for 1 sale on this book is $5.51. The payout for 1 full page read (at the current KENP rate of 0.0047) is $3.89. But each sale represents an average of 2.36 full page reads, so that's $9.18 for the total estimated page reads.

On average, the full value of 1 reported sale is therefore $14.69. Because it's a complete boxed set, I'm not adding sell through and read-through rates to that. But if they apply, calculate them and add them in.

So the true conversion rate isn't 1 every 11.75 clicks. 8 sales represents 18.88 borrows, which is a total of 26.88 conversions off 94 clicks. The ASIN is therefore converting at a rate of 1 every 3.49 clicks.

For an ad spend of $58.10 it's returned $44.08 in sales and $73.44 in page reads for a total return of $117.52.

Now, we have the proper figures for the ROAS formula of ad revenue – ad cost / ad cost x 100. The calculation is therefore:

$$\$117.52 - \$58.10 / \$58.10 \times 100 = 102.27\%$$

That's a nifty return. It's just a smidge over double my investment. If I wanted to, I could up my bid drastically and still make a profit. Or break even or invest in loss depending on my strategy. But in this case, there's no point in upping the bid because I'm already holding the first spot on the Sponsored Product carousel.

A few key points. What's making this possible, even with what many would consider a high bid, is that being a boxed set I can still get sales at a high price point. And, again, being a boxed set, the page count is moderately high. But most of all, it's the conversion rate.

This is the way to win at Amazon ads. You don't need to join a secret Facebook group to discover it. Or pay big bucks for a course from a "guru" who isn't selling better than you are. Write in a longish series (or release boxed sets). Convert well. It's that easy. And it's that hard.

To summarize all this, do the work. Without it, you won't know which keywords to turn off. Or which ones to increase your bid on. Or if they're fulfilling your overarching strategy. You just won't know, and gauging success by making a profit over and above ad spend tells you *nothing* about individual keywords. You could be (and probably are) turning good ones off and leaving bad ones run.

Do the work.

What helps enormously though is keeping a document with all the relevant calculations for each book you advertise nice and handy. Then it only takes a few seconds to do the calculation on a keyword that you're optimizing.

There you have it. I'm not a mathematician. In fact, I hate math with a burning hot passion. I despise it like Maxwell Smart despises KAOS. But it's part of the job. Once you get a handle on it, it doesn't take much time.

I think I have a handle on it. But like I say, math isn't my thing. If you spot a flaw in any of my calculations or assumptions, feel free to join my Facebook group and tell me. Nothing I do or say is set in stone. I'm willing to learn and change if there's a better way.

11. Does Ad Placement Matter?

I'll give you the short answer.

You bet.

There are two different reasons for this. The first is to do with impression volume. It's an easy concept to grasp. The second is to do with CVR, and that's a little more complicated.

First, to impressions.

You are what you eat. And in PPC advertising, you're only as good as the impressions you get. You can do nothing without them. Trying to get a useful number of conversions without the impressions that bring them is like growing carrots in the desert. Without water.

How do you get lots of impressions?

Well, one way is to target widely. I could say indiscriminately because that's what wide targeting is. If you have a product that appeals well to men and women, boys and girls, the young and the old, the readers of thrillers, romance, mysteries, fantasy … then you're a chance of converting to any person who buys books.

Is that you?

I know it's not me. I convert very well, but only within my niche.

What way are we left with then to get lots of impressions? Laser-like targeting is all very well, and sure, it converts at a high rate, but if there are fewer targets how can you get a lot of impressions?

Ad placement is the answer. First, target books (or search terms) with a high sales rank. Only books receiving a lot of impressions themselves are capable of generating a lot of ad impressions. The sales rank (or potential future sales rank) of any potential target is as much a consideration in choosing keywords as anything else.

But each keyword (or search term) can have hundreds and hundreds of ads attached to it. Do each of these ads receive an equal number of impressions?

No. Not at all.

The first page of search results, or the first row of a Sponsored Product carousel, get the majority of views. The deeper you go, the more impressions dry up like an unwrapped sandwich in the fridge.

Even that doesn't really describe it. Trying to appear on the first page or the first row is a gunfight at the O.K. Corral. It's a deadly competition because good advertisers know the first search result on a page gets a lot more impressions than the last on the same page. The same for a Sponsored Product row.

If you want the impressions, you have to be as high up the pecking order of visibility as you can afford to bid.

Do you see now, again and again, how everything comes back to how high you can bid? And that's determined by your relevance, conversion rate and the earning capacity of your book.

The farther back you are, the less impressions you'll get. And without impressions, you can't get clicks. And without clicks, you can't get conversions. Being up the front gives you a chance at a lot of clicks, and if you target well, they're high-converting clicks.

This leads on to the second reason ad placement matters. CVR.

This is more complex though. Ad placement and ad type can, but not always do, impact CVR.

Why?

It's all about prospect behavior. Is their behavior always the same?

No, it's not. It alters. More on this when we come to the ad type chapter.

For the moment, let's stick to the Sponsored Product carousel. It might have twenty to thirty rows. It takes click after click after click to shuffle through them. Most prospects will never reach the end. They'll give up before then. This is why visibility drops rapidly.

But surely, if they go in deeper, a click on row five is just as valuable as a click on row one? Either you've targeted your ad well, or you haven't.

The thing is, the prospect's mental state is different as they keep clicking. They're increasingly likely to become bored or frustrated that they haven't found anything they like. That means they're even more inclined to make snap judgements. This means less time considering cover, title and blurb snippet.

This being the case, they're more likely to make a mistake and click on an ad they might not have a few rows back. This *will* reduce CVR.

But against that, the advertisers who can afford to place their ads high, and have been doing so for a long time, are at a disadvantage. Their ad has already been seen multiple times. The prospect can be bored and frustrated here too, because they're not seeing anything new that they haven't read or haven't already decided not to buy. In this scenario, books farther along can convert better because they're relatively fresh.

This is one of the reasons CVR can fluctuate so mysteriously.

What can you do to find the best placement for your ad? You can test to find the best converting position, and be willing to change ad position over time.

But I like to keep things simple. I aim for the best ad placement I can afford straight up, and drop bid price if it's converting, but not in a way that's meeting my current overarching strategy. If it starts well, but CVR drops over time, I keep lowering the bid price to keep the seesaw where I want it.

This approach maximizes impression volume, but balances it with meeting the chosen advertising strategy.

There's one other force at play though. It's what marketers call the Rule of 7.

Trust marketers to give a mysterious name to it, but it's a very simple concept if you haven't come across it before. Basically, the idea is that a prospect needs contact with the product you're selling multiple times before they decide to buy. Not necessarily seven times at all, but on average something like that.

So the people buying your books have probably seen them floating around a bunch of times before they actually clicked the buy button. Maybe it was an also-bought on the last few books they purchased. They probably saw it on an ad or two as well. Possibly they saw it on another site like Goodreads too.

This feeds strongly into ad placement. The better your ad placement, and the more impressions you get, the more you drive the Rule of 7.

In fact, not only does the Rule of 7 drive sales, it drives a higher CVR. When a book seems to be everywhere, it offers a kind of social proof that it's popular and desirable. People are buying and reading it. The prospect begins to wonder what they're missing out on. When they finally click on it, their interest levels are high.

This is the halo effect at work again, which I wrote about in detail in previous books of this series. It's a subtle predisposition to buy over and above the normal situation.

The Rule of 7 is one of the reasons (out of many) that bestselling authors like Mark Dawson convert well on their ads.

Succeeding as an author is about visibility. But not all visibility is equal. The more you have, the more momentum it gives you.

12. Ad Types and Their Uses

Just like the visibility discussed in the last chapter, not all ad types are equal. Let's run through them, and I'll give you my comments.

Sponsored Product by keyword targeting

This is the most commonly seen ad. Ads appear in the Sponsored Product carousels on a product page. They can also appear in search results after a customer uses the search bar.

The first type is far more valuable than the second.

Why?

Because it's estimated that seventy to ninety percent of sales in the Amazon store come off product pages rather than search results.

Prospects searching for something are either looking for a specific book with an intent of purchase, in which case you're a low chance of having your ad convert. Or they're just searching for a particular book that they know they like, which will serve as an entry point for them to surf through similar titles via the also-bought and Sponsored Product carousels.

None of this means that search result keywords don't work. They can and they do, but they're not the primary means of obtaining conversions. Nowhere near it.

Typical keywords might be an author name, a book name or a general term such as "medical thriller".

An author name keyword might show your ad on a search result, or within any of their books. This includes paperbacks and ebooks. *This is very poor targeting*. As discussed earlier, paperback buyers tend to buy paperbacks and ebook buyers tend to buy ebooks. Amazon will use this type of keyword to promote ebooks to paperback buyers.

Another problem is that many authors don't write in one narrow field. For instance, they might write fiction and nonfiction, fantasy and sci-fi etc. Your ad, once again, is getting shown to prospects with a low chance of buying.

Targeting by a book name removes this last problem, but not the first.

All this is why ad results can be so variable. An author name or book title that worked really well a month ago could be a failure now. How often has that happened to you?

Amazon is showing your ad in a different place despite you using the identical keyword you used before. That's the cause of the variability.

On the plus side, when this type of keyword is working, it works well. You're reaching a large volume of prospects.

To turn now specifically to search term keywords such as "medical thriller", I have to say they're a bit different.

These are highly competitive because it's really only the ads on the first page that get significant visibility. If you want to own a search term such as "contemporary romance" be prepared to pay the big bucks. This is really the invest-in-loss strategy, by necessity. In my experience, the CVR isn't good either.

But test. See how much you have to pay to reach top billing, and see if it works for you in your situation.

There are long tail search terms you can use here as well. For instance, "epic fantasy elves" rather than "epic fantasy". These keywords often tend not to have enough search volume to bother with though.

Maybe there's some middle ground between the highly competitive main keywords and the long tail ones. If there is, I've never found it. But you might.

These search terms, even though they can be extremely specific, are still not well targeted. How do you know if the prospect searching for "sword & sorcery with dragons" is an ebook, paperback, traditionally published or indie reader?

You don't.

But perhaps that doesn't apply to all genres. For instance, reverse harem and litrpg are likely terms searched for by prospects who favor indie ebooks.

The way forward is to look at the advantages and disadvantages of an ad type, and consider how you might use it best to suit your specific situation. Then test your theory.

Conversely, the way backward is to spend no time understanding how an ad type operates, and then follow someone else's advice of what to do or not to do based on what worked for them and their specific situation.

Sponsored Product by product targeting

This type of ad has two options. First, targeting by category. Second, by individual product.

I've already discussed the issues of targeting by category at length. Generally, it's the spaghetti-on-the-wall approach and prone to get you clicks that don't convert.

But, you have to test it for your own books and situation. The more homogenous the category, the more likely it will work for you. The more mixed up it is, the less likely.

Test and trial is the answer here. But kill non-performing ads quickly so they don't drain your credit card. If you get a good one, treasure it! Because category ads offer the one thing that's very hard to get – impression volume.

One more point here. The situation with category ads has slightly improved. Formerly, the US store only allowed you to target category by the "Books/" path. This category path usually means physical books only. Strangely, the UK store always allowed you to target a category by "Books/" or "Ebooks/" at your discretion. But from late 2020 the US allowed category targeting for ebooks as well. As I say, this is an improvement because it allows you more refined targeting.

The second option with this general ad type is the one that I favor and have also discussed at length. It lets you target by individual product, right down to an ASIN. This is the best thing since brownies with marzipan. Target well, and you can convert at 1 in 5, or better. But impression volume is reduced.

Sponsored Product by automatic targeting

Amazon does the work for you here. Basically, this method relies on their algorithms deciding where to place your ads. The main way they can do this is by your metadata.

Results vary, as you would expect. The whole thing is a bit random. The ads seem to work for some, but for others they burn cash quicker than a navy crewman on shore leave.

As always, trial them to see if they work for you.

People frequently use them to find search terms that convert, at least ones that they haven't thought of themselves. I said it was random, and people even report getting sales from customer searches such as "book book book".

No one seems to understand how that works, but they go ahead and use such successful search terms in their manual ads.

This is what I think is happening though. Your book's metadata isn't the only thing available to the algorithms. They also know the prospect's search and buy history. This (I believe) is why totally random search strings such as "book book book" produce results.

Amazon isn't matching your ad up to the prospect's search because of the search term. They're matching it up based on prospect behavior. They *profile* customers. If that person has bought one of your books before, or clicked on one, Amazon is throwing you in front of them again. And the more random the search term the more likely this is to be the case. What else could Amazon do when the search term is so vague that it could legitimately turn up every single book ever published?

This is why adding successful automatic keywords to your manual campaigns can backfire. When you do that, you're trying to match your book to the search term. But that's potentially irrelevant. And manual ads don't seem to utilize the predictive algorithms based on prospect behavior. This is because you're doing the targeting, not Amazon. People also ask why someone would search with a term like "book book book" in the first place. It's pretty random, after all. But I think the prospect is just putting something in to see where it'll take them. They're just diving in somewhere, and anywhere will do, because the aim is to surf Amazon's books and they'll stop when it throws up something interesting.

Lockscreen ads

These ads appear on Kindle E-readers and Fire tablets. It's sometimes said they're the same as the Product

Display ads formerly available via the KDP Ads Dashboard, but now only through an Amazon Advantage account.

I think this is a rookie mistake. The ads are *not* the same, and treating them as such will cost you money.

Lockscreen ads serve on the wakescreen and homepages of Kindles and Fire tablets. Only. The old Product Display ads were split (at Amazon's discretion) between serving in a similar fashion and showing on product pages in the Amazon store. Given the far greater scope for impressions available in the store than on specialized and brand specific reading devices, I'd suggest that most of the old Product Display ads served in the store.

At the heart of good marketing lies an understanding of client behavior. A prospect looking for a book to read in the store has different behavior patterns than someone picking up their reading device to read a book they're part way through.

What I'm getting at is that the first is more likely to buy. Lockscreen ads offer high visibility, but the buying intent of prospects is low.

Another of the problems with Lockscreen ads is that they can show when the device is offline, but a click is still charged even if it can't take the prospect to the product page.

Also, targeting by these ads is very wide and therefore poor.

Basically, few people report success with these ads, and the above are reasons why. However, some people *do* report success. Test and see is the way forward (as always), and the only way to find out what works for you.

One important point to note. Kindle and Fire tablet owners are much more likely to be in KU than other prospects. For this reason, sales can be low but page reads high. When testing, watch the page reads closely.

Sponsored Brand ads

These ads appear in several places, but most prominently above the search results. One word there was important. *Above*. This is incredibly powerful. It brings the potential for a great number of impressions. But, beware.

As you now know, not all impressions are equal. Nor are all clicks. And certainly these ads have a high CTR, but they often don't convert well.

Why?

Once again, look at the mindset and intent of the prospect. If someone types "epic fantasy" in the search bar, what are they looking for? Grimdark? Noblebright? If they type an author or book name, are they seeking paperbacks or ebooks? Insert the variables that apply to your own genre into the equation.

These ads get seen first, and they're big and fancy. That generates a lot of clicks. But it's the targeting that makes or breaks them. Choose targeting where your product is more likely to resonate with the intent of the prospect.

I'm experimenting with them myself (they were only introduced to KDP accounts in late 2020), and I'm getting mixed results. They tend to be expensive and not to convert well. This is in line with the reports of other advertisers. So, be warned that if you're expecting Snow White you might get one of the dwarfs instead.

Product Display ads

This is another ad type currently only available with an Amazon Advantage account. They can be set up by product or interest, and each mode allows good targeting. But the ads can display in a number of places.

As you now know, ad placement matters. Unfortunately, because ad placement is at Amazon's discretion, you'll get mixed results. If the ad shows in a favorable spot, for instance the banner style ad in the middle of the page directly above the also-bought row, you're a high chance of good results. Elsewhere, not so much.

You know how I work now.

Why? That's the question to ask.

The other most prominent place for these ads, or *seemingly* most prominent because the ad is large, is on the right-hand side of the product page.

This may come as a surprise to you, although it won't if you're a professional PPC marketer, but the right panel of a webpage is just about invisible. It's the worst possible place to put an ad. In fact, in my former government job, if we wanted to hide something we'd put it on the right. For instance, if we wanted people to write to us instead of phone, we'd place the address on the left or the middle and the phone number on the right.

If you doubt me on this, and you should – never take anyone's word for it in this business because this is the gold rush days of indie publishing and there are frauds and hustlers everywhere pretending knowledge and trying to separate you from your cash – Google "heatmap of a webpage" and look at the images.

It's not foolproof, and there are ways to draw the gaze right, but this is about the worst possible place to put an ad.

Small wonder that few people report success with this type of ad. If you have a startling cover, it's a better chance of drawing the prospect's gaze. Possibly, those who report success with these ads have that going for them.

But this right-hand placement has more problems still. It's not consistent. Sometimes the ad appears in line with the also-bought carousel. This is good because the line of movement of the prospect's gaze goes toward it. Other times, it's placed higher in no man's land. This is bad.

In either situation, the ad is right next to the scroll bar that people use on a notebook to scroll down the page. This leaves the ads open to accidental clicks. And those ads that display in line with the end of the also-bought carousel are smack bang beside the arrow used to shuffle through the carousel. Again, accidental clicks are more likely.

To summarize, this ad type generally offers low visibility and high potential for accidental clicks.

I'm not suggesting for a moment that Amazon deliberately puts the ad in the places they do to take advantage of accidental clicks, but I'd sure bet there are a fair few of them.

None of this is an issue for Sponsored Product ads. They have high visibility and only the last book of the row is a chance of an accidental click by being next to the shuffle arrow. So, if you're running Sponsored Product ads and your book is in that spot, bid a few cents more!

That's about all I have to say on the different ad types. But I have one more general comment stemming from all this.

I hope it's clear that succeeding with Amazon ads uses a bit of math and data analysis. But no matter that you're a brilliant mathematician or world-class data analyst, advertising requires much, much more than that. It requires marketing skills. It's all about understanding prospect behavior and mindset, webpage design and the science of PPC advertising.

Dig deep to discover the truth. Labor under correct knowledge. Don't get caught up too much in data analysis.

It's a tool, but just one of many. If you do, you'll miss the forest for the trees.

13. What's at Fault? Product or Ad?

This is a difficult chapter. In a way, it's not about Amazon ads at all.

The thing with advertising is that you can't create something from nothing. Marketing follows certain laws in the same way that the laws of physics apply to the universe. You can't create matter without energy. You can't create energy without matter. Energy and matter are inextricably linked.

This is a roundabout way of easing you into the idea that no matter how good you are at advertising, and no matter how big your budget, it's pushing water uphill to try to sell a book that doesn't resonate with an audience. Likewise, no matter how good the book is, it's rare these days for one to take off without significant advertising spend.

That's good and bad news for people who run Amazon ads. If your book resonates, everything will be that little bit easier. You're not pushing water uphill but forward over flat ground. If you gain advertising expertise, you can begin to count on gravity pulling the water at the same time as you push. When you're pushing water downhill, you're on the advertising gravy train.

But what if your book doesn't resonate?

This is hard. Writers pour their heart into a story. It's them. It's the *real* them. It's their soul, exposed for all the world to see.

But if you're not selling, you have to ask why. Is your craft not good enough yet? Are there major faults with your blurb?

Advertising helps you identify the problem. It gives your book visibility. If you're targeting books very much like your own, and you're getting impressions and clicks but a low CVR, it's time to look hard at your blurb and the first few chapters of the book. There lies the problem.

Book two in this series gave expert advice on blurbs. A later book in this series will tackle the craft of fiction itself, and how to use the same behavioral insights that drive blurbs and sales copy to ignite the story itself.

One final thought. There's a difference between getting impressions, clicks and conversions, and not profiting … and not being able to get conversions. In the first scenario, what you need to make advertising work is a longer series or boxed set. In the second, it's the product itself.

Take heart. There was a time when Shakespeare had to learn his craft too.

14. Should You Use Dynamic Bids?

Dynamic bidding can be down only, or up and down. Either way, it gives Amazon more control.

Is this a good thing?

Maybe.

First, what this process relies on is the algorithms. In turn, they rely on an accumulation of data about how the book performs. They then make a prediction and increase or lower your bid according to their calculation of your likelihood of a sale.

That sounds complex. Let me put it another way.

Amazon makes a guess.

That's all it is. It's not to be relied on.

However, the older your book is, the more the ad has run and has had time to accumulate data. Then, the guess becomes more accurate.

So, my advice is *never* to start an ad with either of the forms of dynamic bidding. Back your own judgement instead. Is your targeting good? Have you figured out the maximum you're willing to bid? Run with that and use the fixed bidding option. Then do your own optimizing as you start to get enough data.

But after a while, I'd shift to dynamic up and down bidding and watch the results. If it's an improved ROAS, keep things going. If not, flip back to fixed.

How long is a while?

It's impossible to know how much data Amazon needs to make good predictions, if they can even make them at all. But as a rough benchmark, I'd say 25,000 impressions.

My personal experience with dynamic bidding is that it gives mixed results. I'd say most advertisers would be in the same boat.

What dynamic bidding is really trying to do is optimize. But at the end of the day, I'd rather do that myself. If someone is going to play on that seesaw, I want it to be me and not Amazon.

But as always, test and trial. Just try not to get caught up in the fancy schmancy gimmickry of the ad dashboard. People get all fixated on the bells and whistles Amazon is beginning to give us as the platform improves, but this little stuff rarely makes much difference. Keep your mind firmly on the core principles of success. Good targeting. Bidding high enough to get traction. And having a book "package" big enough that you can afford that higher bid.

15. How to Scale and Why it's Hard

The methods of scaling are intricately tied to the good PPC practices we've already covered. First, find as many relevant keywords as possible. Ensure they have a good enough sales rank to produce impressions. The higher the sales rank, the greater the potential impressions. Then, obtain the best ad positioning possible on those keywords – that you can afford.

This is not a cheap process. The CPC on high ranking keywords is, well, high. This is because they're competitive. And they're competitive for good reason. Other advertisers know their worth, and they're prepared to bid high to benefit from them. It's not Amazon driving up bid amounts. It's authors.

In a tactical sense, you're in a bidding war trying to get good positions on those impression-generating keywords. But in a strategic sense, it's not about the bid, and this is where even veteran indie publishers can miss a trick. It's about building up the "package" that allows you to bid high in the first place. It's about the long series, the big box set and the conversion rate.

Conversion rate in turn is decided by how good your craft is as a fiction writer. And how good your sales copy is in the backmatter as a copywriter.

Optimizing the sales copy at the back of the book is vital. Please don't underestimate this. It directly contributes to buy and read-through rates of your books. In turn, this influences your chances of success with Amazon ads.

Unfortunately, there are as many myths, misplaced calls to action and bad advice floating around about backmatter as there are about blurbs.

Back to scaling. The above are the raw ingredients of success, but there are other factors that influence things in a less controllable way.

The Rule of 7

I touched on this earlier in the book. The more your book is seen, whether in an ad or elsewhere, the greater the chance of a purchase.

Often, prospects don't buy the first time they see something. They usually see it multiple times before they buy, and their interest level grows over time. The more something is seen, the greater credibility it tends to have.

This means that the more you sell organically, the better your ads will perform. The more ad visibility you have, the better your organic sales. They feed into each other, and the sum of their total is greater than just their individual parts added together.

Success breeds success.

This is great when you're on a roll, but in a slowdown it makes it harder to scale. It is, however, a reason to make sure you're advertising strongly at a time when you have a new release with a lot of visibility. Especially if you're advertising on Amazon where you know your targets will see you. Other platforms can feed into the Rule of 7, but not so strongly as Amazon.

Incidentally, although I made it fairly clear in the chapter on the different types of ads that I'm not much of a fan of Lockscreen, Category or Product Display ads, these do increase the effectiveness of Sponsored Product ads. They feed into the Rule of 7, but (in my view) that's not enough to justify them. They should still pay their own way.

Sales rank

This, I think, is the biggest factor of all when it comes to scaling.

Amazon reward sales. The more you sell, the more they push you toward prospects. The less you sell, the less they push you.

In terms of Amazon ads specifically, I know I can get ten times the number of impressions and conversions on a book when it sells really well compared to the same book months later.

Sales rank is the secret sauce. It's rocket fuel for your ads. It ignites them like *nothing* else.

But if you don't have it, you don't have it. You can't create it with ads alone.

There's not much you can do about this situation. At least not with ads. Ads are just a tool at your disposal, and one of many.

This is why it's important to hone all aspects of your craft as a fiction writer, and the same for your marketing efforts such as blurb, backmatter, covers etc. And when a book takes off, enjoy the ride that advertising can give it. This is the best time to advertise and to take advantage of the situation.

When your book has lower rank, keep up the advertising. But expect much, much smaller results. There are only so many places for an ad to be shown, and Amazon is going to give most of those spots to books that are selling well right *now*, not ones that did in the past or might in the future.

The opposite phenomenon of scaling is this: ads that were doing really well dying. This happens a lot. As the sales rank of your book decays over time, Amazon's willingness to serve it in ads decreases.

If you were Amazon, what would you rather show a customer in an ad? A book selling like hotcakes? Or one with a low sales rank?

Patience is the strategy here, grasshopper. Work toward building organic sales. Work toward having a good mailing list. Work toward the best understanding you can get of how to launch and promote your backlist.

Then pounce when you get the chance.

16. Does Ad Budget Impact Ad Performance?

There's a theory.

It goes like this. Set a daily budget of $1,000.00. Maybe $10,000.00. Or even $100,000.00. This is supposed to ensure all your keywords serve well. The algorithms try to figure out which money out of *all* the Amazon advertisers' budgets to spend, and if your budget is high, your ad gets preference. And of course, Amazon is never going to spend all that money. Spend remains within normal levels, even if ad service improves.

Is it true?

People have tried it. There's a lot of talk about it in certain circles. But I've never seen any evidence this works better than a hundred-dollar budget.

I've tried it, but it made no difference.

If you're willing to risk it, give it a go. Maybe it'll work for you.

There's a risk mitigation strategy that goes with this. You're supposed to set your bids low so that if for some reason Amazon does give you an avalanche of impressions, and you get corresponding clicks, you won't get bankrupted. The problem with this though is that it's like pressing the accelerator and brake of your car at the same time.

Low bids defeat the purpose of a high budget. But they *are* protective in this scenario. Perhaps the best way to do it is to leave bids as they are and increase budget gradually. If the ad takes off, this gives you the chance to monitor its effectiveness. If it's working well, you might want to increase *both* budget and bids. If not, you can switch it off before it costs too much money.

Personally, I have zero faith in the whole thing. It certainly made no difference to me. But the idea persists, so I thought I'd share it with you. My suspicion is that it's a tactic Amazon sellers used to use effectively years ago, and then Amazon wised up and changed their algorithms to close the loophole. Amazon does this a lot. You can see why in this case too. Being client-centric as they are, they want ads to show on relevance rather than trickery.

Whatever you do though, for any ad in any situation, make sure there's enough money in the budget to service all the keywords. If you have an ad with hundreds of keywords and a budget of $5.00, it's impossible for Amazon to show the ad across them all. This is like trying to turn the water tap on to fill a bucket, but pressing your hand over the outlet at the same time to stop the water coming out.

Related to the high-budget strategy is a slightly different one. You can try it with or without raising the budget. This theory goes that you can force Amazon to give you more impressions by setting an end date to the ad only a few days away instead of weeks or months.

Does this work?

I suspect it works. A little bit. Again, trial it for yourself and see. But the problem with it is that it's high maintenance. You have to keep going back into the ad frequently to adjust the end date.

Frankly, I couldn't be bothered.

It should be clear by now that there's no cheap trick, hack or bamboozlement to hoodwink Amazon's algorithms into giving you a greater slice of the impression pie than they want to give you.

The search for a party trick that will shortcut you a road to success is what keeps your mind off the things that really are effective, but aren't easy.

Do the work. In the end, *that's* the shortcut.

17. Should You Use Ad Copy?

Amazon gives us a choice with some ad types to use, or not to use, ad copy.

It's interesting that they do this. Is it to offer us convenience and make it as frictionless as possible for authors to advertise?

Perhaps. It *is* a revenue stream for Amazon after all.

The UK store takes this further. For some ad types, which are otherwise identical to what's served in the US store, ad copy is simply not an option. They've removed the possibility of it.

Why?

It could be an ease of use thing. But I don't think so. I think their data shows that the thumbnail cover on the ad carousel, the star rating and the price are the most influential determinants of which ad gets a click and which doesn't.

The internet retail world is one of snap decisions. Clicks are made, or not made, in a heartbeat. The world of the ad carousel is even harsher. It's like a hyperactive mouse with a caffeine high running in a wheel.

The heartbeat of that mouse is fast. So are the decisions made on ads. Fast decisions are often poor decisions, and this feeds into the reasons that poor targeting can still lead to clicks, but explains why those clicks don't convert. Not all clicks are equal. At all.

So, what this is getting at is that I deduce from Amazon's decisions on the topic that many prospects don't read the ad copy.

This reduces its importance.

But it doesn't eliminate it. Obviously, some people do read it. How many is impossible to say, but it must still be a significant amount.

For that reason, we should use it. At least when Amazon gives us the option.

Once again, do the work. And in this case the work isn't very hard. It comes with a benefit too.

For that percentage of prospects who do read the ad copy, it enables better discernment. Covers can convey genre, but subgenre is a bit harder. Having copy that further refines the message of the cover will increase click quality. It will save you money.

What should this little blurb snippet say?

Space is at a premium. Try not to explain much about the story. Write something that hits the subgenre tropes at a glance. Keep it simple and obvious. Layer it with some kind of hook, preferably an open loop (a teaser).

What you shouldn't do is use a tagline or opening sentence from your blurb.

Why?

Because you want your ad to resonate with the blurb. You want a prospect going from the first to the second to feel that they haven't miss-clicked. If they get jarred by something completely different, they're going to be suspicious and less likely to buy. You want resonance not jarring. But most especially, you don't want to *bore* them.

Using your blurb's tagline as ad copy makes the prospect read the same thing twice, only a few seconds apart. This diffuses its power. It's boring. Whatever reaction it provoked the first time is only a pale imitation the second.

Come up with ad copy that signals subgenre, teases and resonates with the blurb while still being different. It'll serve you well.

There's another theory with ad copy. It applies to blurbs too. The theory goes that Amazon uses this metadata to help establish relevance.

So, if you're advertising on a target book – let's call it *Elf Warrior*, and you include "elf" or "warrior" in the blurb and ad copy of your own book, Amazon will assign you a higher relevance score against your target.

Like I say, it's a theory. Don't take it for fact.

For myself, I'm satisfied there's no substance to it. But let's assume it's true. Even so, there are other factors involved in the relevance score. Such as CTR, CVR and your backend search terms (the keywords you use on publishing your book). If Amazon operates like they usually do, these factors will be weighted. Some will be given higher influence than others.

You can be sure that keywords in the ad copy and blurb are weighted far less than actual responsive client behavior such as CTR.

And keyword stuffing is a dangerous business. It can (and usually will) reduce the effectiveness of your copywriting.

By all means try it. But be careful. Do it smoothly and naturally. A good blurb or some good ad copy is far more valuable to you than a marginal (if any) boost to relevancy.

For what it's worth, I've tried it. My results were better without it.

But as always, test it yourself. See what happens for you in your own situation.

There are a few other tactics at play. You'll see this especially on books advertised in the Top 100. They'll have the "If you liked X you'll like Y" comment, or one of its variations. I think this is definitely worth a shot. It plays right into the fast decisions going on with ad clicks because it's the most succinct way possible of describing what a book is like.

It's never worked for me (not on Amazon, though it has on BookBub), but it might be genre dependent. There's no harm in trying it.

The other tactic you'll see, again in the Top 100 list (it's the best place to study tactics) is mentioning something like "Free in KU."

This last tactic seems to me to be pushing too close to the edge of Amazon's TOS when it comes to ad wording (they don't like price messages in ads) but given that ads are manually considered and approved or rejected by Amazon, it appears they're okay with it.

18. Advertising Later Books in a Series

Most people only seem to advertise book one of a series. I get this, because book ones are more responsive. Later books are hit and miss with advertising.

But it's leaving candies in the candy jar.

Look at Amazon's Top 100 chart. Look at the ads on any of these books They're chockers with later books in a series.

The top 100 is a dog eat dog world. The authors with books there, which are often the only authors who can afford to advertise there, know stuff. If they're advertising later books in the series, it's because it works.

I could have mentioned this in the scaling chapter. It *is* a type of scaling, but I didn't because it involves using a separate book. Be that as it may, advertising later books in the series can put people on to book one. Or, it might trigger people to buy the later book because they've read all the others in the series and didn't know the newest one was out.

Either way, you get greater visibility in the store than is possible with just book one alone. In fact, if you advertise two books in the series you get potentially twice the exposure. If you advertise three … well, you get my drift.

But as I said above, subsequent books rarely attract the interest that book one of a series does. They appear to have worse CTRs and worse CVRs. Why that should be, I'm not sure. Perhaps because the prospect knows that clicking on that ad will really necessitate a second click back to book one (if they're new to the series). After all, no one will buy a later book without buying book one.

Nothing is set in stone though. I've had good ads for later books in a series. Sometimes, they take off.

At any rate, if you write in a series, try to advertise as many books as you can within the series. Maybe books 2, 3 and 5 don't respond, but books 1, 4 and 6 do well. This will help you scale. And, if your series branding is good, it'll also feed into the Rule of 7.

19. Defensive Advertising

This is talked about from time to time. Generally, it's discussed in relation to Sponsored Brand ads.

The idea works like this. Let's say you're Mark Dawson. You're pretty well known and *lots* of people read your books. That makes you a prime advertising target. Other authors will create an ad, using your name or books, and place it to try to poach buyers away from you and to them instead. Especially if they write similar books.

There's no doubt this can work. A Sponsored Brand ad is pretty fancy, and it displays at the top of the page above the search results. So the competitor gets seen before the actual author the prospect was searching for.

Enter defensive advertising. If you're Mark Dawson, you can place your *own* Sponsored Brand ad against yourself. If you bid high enough, the prospect sees your ad first. Then they see your organic listing.

This is pretty neat. You've defended your territory, and saved some poached sales.

But if you dig deep, is it really a good idea?

I'll be honest. I don't know. Mark Dawson is actually one of the chief proponents of the idea, and he's one of the most influential indie adviser out there. But my philosophy is to question everything, and I don't think he'd disagree with that worldview, especially in this industry where a lot of bad advice (not from him) is bandied around.

These are the issues.

You certainly save sales that would otherwise have been poached. It's impossible to put a number on them though.

You also certainly pay for clicks on your ad by prospects who searched you out with the strong intent of buying your book, and who would not have been swayed by a competitor's ad. That prospect just happened to click your ad rather than your organic listing. But again, it's impossible to put a number on them.

So defensive advertising will simultaneously lose you money and make you money. The question is, out of these competing forces, which one is the greater?

I don't know the answer. I don't believe anyone does.

To muddy the waters even more, prospects could use a search term like "Mark Dawson" for two very different reasons. Firstly, they might have just finished one of his books and thought it was a ripper, so they're looking for more from him. Or, they've read all his books and want a new author, but one similar to him. So they search him out with the intention of surfing his also-boughts.

My tactic in a situation like this, where I don't know the answer, is not to invest in advertising. I'd rather redirect my budget to where I can get clearer results as to whether I'm making money or losing money.

But that's just me. What would you do? Do you know a means of estimating profit against loss here?

Those are serious questions. If you know the best way forward, please contact me and let me know! I *hate* not knowing.

There's another aspect to this. I've only ever heard the tactic spoken of in relation to Sponsored Brand ads, but something similar happens with Sponsored Product ads too.

Someone clicks on your book, reads your blurb, and then gets distracted by an ad beneath it. They end up buying that book instead of yours.

I'd suggest, in this case, if the prospect read your blurb but bought another book anyway, you were never much chance with them. So placing an ad for your own book on its own product page is (probably) a waste of time.

But what about a different book of your own? Maybe book one of a different series? That could be a good defensive strategy to poaching.

Like I say, I don't know the answers here. I wish I did. But I bring up these issues for your consideration. You should be aware of them so that you can make up your own minds on the best way forward.

20. Is Keyword-finding Software a Good Idea?

There are software apps that find keywords and spare you time and effort in researching them yourself.

Are they a good idea?

At least for indie authors, my opinion is firmly in the no camp.

My reasoning is pretty simple.

It's said in farming circles that the best fertilizer is the farmer's footsteps. This is because it means the farmer is always out and about, keeping an eye on things and doing what needs to be done when it needs doing. He knows his fields. He knows the state of the fences. He knows what weeds are coming up. He knows how his animals are faring, and what the weather is doing, or likely to do soon. He has an intimate knowledge of the land that he's custodian of.

If you know any farmers, and have been out on the land with them, you'll know what I mean. They have eyes in the back of their head. They see the same things that you see, but they *notice* and you don't.

PPC marketing is similar. It requires an intimate knowledge of the retail platform's environment.

What does this mean to you, as an indie author?

It means you should know your niche like the back of your hand. What authors are doing well? Which ones not so well? Who is advertising? Who isn't? Who has a new release? What are the styles of the successful authors? Which ones are a close match to you? Which ones appear close superficially, but when you dig are different?

There's another way to put this. *Who are your best targets?* No software can tell you that. None. Not even close.

Like most shortcuts, software will cost you in the end. Better to do the work yourself. By doing the work and finding your own keywords, you see what's in front of everyone, but you *notice*.

21. Is Ad Fatigue Real?

There are those who say ads die.

Do they?

Not really.

At least, not in the way those people say. They seem to just take it as a given that most ads won't work. And that they'll flicker to life briefly for a few days, maybe a week, and then fade away again.

This is a frequent symptom of the spaghetti-on-the-wall approach. In truth, many of those ads don't die. Amazon stops serving them, or suppresses them, because they're not giving a good customer experience. And how could they? They're not targeted to try to meet customers' needs.

This is a sin against good marketing.

Okay. Maybe I'm getting a bit strident.

Or not. You decide.

The point is, that type of ad doesn't do you much good. Amazon comes out worse for wear too. At the end of the day, they have more to lose than you do.

So bad ads get stifled. Especially bad Sponsored Product ads. Product Display ads are half invisible, so I think Amazon shows more lenience there. Or maybe the bad ads get shuffled to the right of the screen while the good ones get prime position in the middle of the screen.

But there is a limit, even for good ads. Amazon has a massive pool of book buyers. The pool for each subgenre is obviously much smaller (but still pretty massive). But of that pool, only a certain percentage will click on ads. Many people run ad blockers, and many just refuse to click on an ad.

What sized pool are we left with?

It's impossible to know. It'll vary by subgenre. But one thing's for sure – it's finite.

At some point an ad will have garnered the clicks of those who are most attracted to it. Then of those who are somewhat attracted. CTR and CVR will gradually drop. On top of this, the book's rank will drop too. The ad will be served less, and even when it's served, it won't respond as well.

This is called ad fatigue. If you like, it's the phase after the Rule of 7 has played out.

There's not a lot you can do. Adjacent targeting, if you can get it to work, helps. It finds you a fresh, or fresher, audience.

You can alter ad copy, but I don't think that's going to do much. The cover tells the prospect at a glance that it's a book they've already bought, or seen before and rejected. They're unlikely to read the blurb-snippet, new or old.

You can change the cover itself. This *will* work. Sort of. Your CTR is likely to go up. But your CVR is still likely to drop. This is because you'll be getting a lot of clicks from people who've already read the book but didn't know because of the new cover.

Turning ads off for several months to allow a break, and turning those same ads on again so that they retain relevance (new ads start from scratch) is a tactic worth exploring.

22. False Gurus and the Quick Buck

We're still in the goldrush days of indie publishing. To be sure, the time when someone could upload a few books without advertising and make millions are over. But indie publishing is still maturing. It hasn't stabilized yet, nor found its final form. If there is such a thing. But it *has* transformed from an artist's world into a business world. More and more, the artists who are having commercial success run their indie venture as a business and adopt business practices.

PPC advertising is one of those practices. And like many of the others, it's not the natural habitat of writers. Because of this, there's a tremendous thirst for knowledge. Writers want to know *how* to do things in this new world.

But for all the changes, indie publishing is still in an early phase. We work in an environment where some (by no means all) of the "gurus" out there charging hefty prices for how-to books and courses don't know what they're doing. They're incompetent. They've been able to position themselves as experts because there are comparatively few authorities giving advice, and the knowledge base of the audience who thirst for information isn't yet as high as it will be.

That knowledge base is rising though. And fast. The indie world is bubbling along into a new phase. Within five years some of these gurus will be exposed for what they are. Pretenders, earning a fast buck off the dreams of authors.

I don't want to paint you a false picture. There's lots of good advice out there too. There are people who release how-to books and run courses who know exactly what they're doing. They're brilliant.

As always, it's a case of buyer beware. Choose your sources of information wisely.

In respect to Amazon ads, look to see that the person you're taking advice from on how to run them is actually advertising themselves. Look to see that they're successful as an author. Ignore the hype, and look at their sales rank. Most of all, broaden your horizon beyond the restrictive author world and read blogs about PPC advertising and watch YouTube videos from marketers selling and advertising products other than books.

There's a wealth of information out there in the wider world, untapped by authors. Pick up on what successful advertisers do and how they think.

This is the way I learned most of what I know, and then I applied it to my own publishing business. To be honest, my professional expertise lies in the persuasion side of marketing and not at all in PPC advertising. But it's learnable, if you follow good advice and do the work.

Conversely, if you follow bad advice you can work and work and work, but your labor will never bear results.

How can you identify good PPC advice?

Look for the patterns. Start with the wider world of PPC advertising. It has two decades of history. Billions of dollars are spent each year by professional marketers. They have things refined to an art and a science. Learn what they say. Understand the concepts they embrace and the tactics they use.

Study the information provided by successful indie authors too. Test the advice you receive in the author world against real PPC experts. Does the author advice conform to this greater body of knowledge? If it does, you're on a tried and tested path.

Likewise, be wary of oddball approaches. That comes from pretenders who know nothing about PPC advertising.

Authors tend to think books are special. But in an advertising sense, they're just another product like shoes or garlic crushers.

Amazon's PPC platform is much like Facebook's or Google's. It's not the same, but the similarities are far greater than the differences. Within Amazon itself, the differences between other products and books are miniscule.

There's one difference though that it pays to keep in mind when interpreting PPC advice for the Amazon store in general and applying it to books.

Most products are one off, or irregular buys. How frequently do you need to buy a garlic crusher? Once every five years. Or ten? More?

With that type of product, the Amazon sellers are always selling to a new customer. Success in advertising comes from getting higher in the search results and on competitors' also-boughts. Then they try to stay there. And really, the pecking order is fairly stable.

In this sense, books are different. Customers buy new books frequently. Once they've read a book, they move onto the next, which will probably be one of the author's competitors.

So a book's sales rank isn't held steady by a stream of new buyers like a garlic crusher. It has a flood of sales instead, lifting it high on release, and then sales decay.

This means that book sales follow a bell curve. This is different from a garlic crusher, which might retain a similar level of sales month after month and year after year. The end result of this is that it's more important to advertise when you have a new release. Push it hard to lift the crest of the bell curve as high as you can. This aligns your organic sales with your PPC sales, and the two forces work together to stimulate the recommendation engine.

Trying to advertise a book that's had and lost its peak of organic sales is like urging a horse to run faster once it's already finished the race.

Note, this doesn't mean you can't advertise your backlist. It just means you can't expect as good a result. It also doesn't mean that a book rising high again because of a new release in the series doesn't respond well to advertising either.

I think this book has given you a firm grounding in advanced PPC strategies. But I urge you to learn more. There's a wealth of resources out there. Here are a few that I recommend.

Mark Dawson comes first to my mind. It's not a personal recommendation because I haven't done his courses. But I have listened to some of his webinars and podcasts. He knows what he's talking about. He's not a pretender.

In terms of other indie authors, I suggest joining a Facebook group called Authors Optimizing Amazon And Facebook Ads – Support Group. It's a great free resource on the subject.

Deb Potter is a member of the above group. She's released the only other book on Amazon ads that I recommend. You'll find many other regular posters with insightful comments too.

Brian Meeks also has a Facebook group on the subject. As it happens, I disagree with Brian on pretty much every point. He takes a data analyst approach (which is his background). I'm firmly in the marketing camp, and they're two entirely separate fields of expertise.

As I say, I disagree with all his views, passionately, but there's no harm in joining his group. Hearing and discussing different opinions gives perspective. You can't just follow someone blindly. Question what they say. Verify. Research the alternatives. Weigh everything up and make your *own* choices. Perspective is an invaluable tool here.

Bryan Cohen also runs a group and an Amazon ads challenge. The ad challenge is free, but it funnels you toward his paid courses. My suggestion here is to look at the sales rank of his own books. Same with Brian Meeks. If you think they're selling well, then perhaps you can learn from them.

There are far, far more resources available on Amazon ads from a general selling perspective. Book sales are a miniscule part of Amazon's business. But the PPC advertising platform is virtually identical for non-book products as it is for book products.

I highly recommend searching out this much bigger world. It's massive. It's full of people running multi-million-dollar businesses. It dwarfs the publishing scene.

YouTube is a good place to start. Just search a topic of interest such as "Amazon ads relevance" or whatever topic you're researching.

Personally, I like the Ad Badger channel. The Sellics channel is also useful. So too is the PPC Entourage channel. There are hundreds of others. Look out in particular for presentations and interviews with Cherie Yvette.

Hit Google up as well. There's an abundance of free information out there. Some of it is of the highest quality. Some not. You have to be discerning.

When is that not the case, grasshopper?

23. Ads Versus Spam

In some ways, this is the most important chapter of the book. Here, you come to the great divide in marketing, and face two diametrically opposed choices.

Pro marketers have a definition for marketing. It's connecting a person to a product they're likely to want. Not too complicated, is it? This is also known as selling to a warm audience. It has benefits, such as converting at a higher rate.

Spam is another type of marketing. It's shady. It belongs to the underbelly of the advertising world. It's the haunt of foreign princes who want to give you millions, beautiful girls who want to befriend you and pills that will solve any problem.

The main concept of spamming can be summed up like this. *Get the sale any way you can.* This is selling to a cold audience. It's hoping that someone suffers from ringing in the ears and is interested in the cure. Proponents don't care if they spam a thousand other inboxes as long as they also reach the few people suffering the malady.

Selling to a cold audience has a lower conversion rate. This is because the person being spammed doesn't want the product. Or doesn't trust it. But every once in a while spam hits the jackpot and finds a person who forgot to engage their BS radar, or is actually interested.

Let's summarize those two strategies.

Good marketing connects a person to a product they're likely to want. It has a high conversion rate because it's targeting a warm audience.

Spamming tries to get the sale any way it can. It has a low conversion rate because it's selling to a cold audience.

There's a consequence to these approaches. Good marketing can pay a higher price to get attention because it converts more often. Spamming converts badly so it spreads out over many cold targets to seek the elusive jackpots. Consequently, spend, per target, must be low.

Let's apply these ideas to Amazon ads. An advertiser following good marketing principles will have a small number of ads. Each will have a small number of targets. Everything they do is focused on finding readers who want to read a book like theirs. Because they're connecting their book to readers likely to want to read it, their conversion rate is higher. This means they can afford higher bids and buy more visibility for the same price.

An advertiser following spamming principles will have a large number of ads. Each ad will have a large number of targets. Everything they do is focused on finding a jackpot reader out of the blue. Because they're putting their ad in front of readers less interested in their book, their conversion rate is low. This means they have to bid low and constantly churn out new ads to try to scale up their visibility.

You'll see gurus propounding both strategies. Those who favor spamming never call it that though. They'll say they believe in relevance, but if something walks like a duck, and quacks like a duck … you can call it Donald.

Obviously, Amazon is aware of these competing strategies. We know which one they favor. They prefer not to spam their customers. This is why they enforce a relevance score.

The relevance score reflects reader engagement. The more readers click, the more engaged they are. The ad is being shown to people more likely to buy. Conversely, if the ad isn't getting a lot of clicks, Amazon starts to worry it's annoying customers and treats it as spam, shutting it down after a week or so. This is why people who use the method have to continually start new ads.

There's another point of difference. Workload. A smaller group of warm targets is easy to find and manage. A larger group is time consuming to find and manage.

So far, this has all been black and white. Because it really is black and white. At least for the most part. There are a few exceptions though where wider targeting can sometimes work.

Nonfiction is an example. People tend to read it because they're trying to solve a problem. For instance, their back hurts. They might be looking at an Agatha Christie book when your ad pops up, but if it looks like it solves their back problem they become a warm audience. Because lots of people suffer back issues, your random audience is a bit warmer than usual.

With fiction, people mostly read in niches. If someone is looking at an Agatha Christie book and they see your ad for a fairy tale retelling, they're likely to remain a cold audience. However, the exception here tends to be thrillers. Thrillers have a wide demographic appeal. Male and female. Young and old. Thrillers are "mainstream" and not niche like most other genres.

These are exceptions. Even so, these folks will likely find their conversion rate when targeting widely is low.

There are more ramifications of this great divide. Loose targeting associates you with random or semi random books. Tight targeting on higher ranking books shifts you up their also-boughts. This creates organic visibility for you on a warm audience and generates sales over and above your ads. Spamming never does that.

24. A Master Checklist of Success

I've called this a checklist. I'm never happy with that term. A checklist doesn't replace an understanding of all the material covered in this book.

But it does serve as a summary, so I offer it here for your use.

Determine which core strategy (small-scale profit, higher-scale profit, breaking even or investing in loss) applies. This decision shapes the rest of your choices. Unless you're already successful at Amazon ads, I suggest starting with small-scale profit.

Find your very best core targets, perhaps 50 to 100. They should be like for like, including indie for indie and subgenre for subgenre, but not limited to that. See the text for details. But in short, they should be the closest match possible to the book you're advertising. They should also have a good sales rank, so they're capable of generating impressions.

Make sure the book you're advertising isn't already suffering from ad fatigue. A new release will work best.

Set up a Sponsored Product ad, and target by ASIN or keyword. Sponsored Product ads are the flagship ad type with the greatest chance of success.

Estimate your conversion rate.

Estimate the real value of a sale to you.

Calculate the maximum CPC you can afford, based on your conversion rate and the real value of a sale, bearing in mind your chosen core strategy.

Set bids *slightly* higher than the maximum CPC, because the CPC is usually lower than actual bids.

Write good ad copy. Signal subgenre. Include a hook. It should resonate with the blurb, but on no account be the same.

Make sure your budget is high enough to fund clicks across your targets.

As data comes in, optimize. Trust Amazon to accurately report conversions on the ads dashboard, but give them time. Profit is the goal, not perfect data. Don't wait for statistical relevance. That will send you broke or force you into the low-bid spaghetti-on-the-wall model.

Determine which method of measuring ad results to use. Choose wisely. It's better to get poor results, recognize that, and find the remedy than to use the comparison method (total ad spend compared to total profit) which serves to make the adviser who taught you look good but hides defects in your practices.

Remember that marketing is a feedback loop. Learn from any mistakes, refine and try again. Seize opportunities with keywords that are working. If there's a leak in sales, find it. Is it the ad? Or is it the product?

When successful at this approach, consider upgrading to one of the next core marketing strategies, depending on your publishing goals and situation.

When successful, try to scale by targeting more widely, but still target well. Allow for the possibility of lower CVR, and bid lower accordingly. Try advertising other books in the same series.

Scaling even further may include trying traditionally published authors.

Scaling may also include trying different ad types. Proceed with *extreme* caution.

Continue to optimize. Remember that perfect data is the enemy of profit.

Rinse and repeat.

Ask questions and discuss your results in one of the Facebook groups devoted to this. It will help you troubleshoot problems.

Keep learning! A journey of a thousand miles begins with a single footstep.

There you have it. Like I say, it's no replacement for coming to grips with the concepts in this book. Understanding them requires more than ticking off items in a checklist. Still, I think you'll find it useful.

25. A Facebook Group to Seek out Best Practice

We've come a long way since the beginning of this book, yes? But all the way through has been the same guiding belief that sparked life into all the previous books of the series: success stems from questioning standard advice and striving for best practice.

Best practice, like Fox Mulder's truth, is out there. But no one person grasps it all. Still less do people share. When they discover a rare truth, they tend to keep it to themselves because it was hard-won knowledge. It's the pretenders who disseminate the most information, the most loudly.

But not always.

There's another way. Sometimes writers *do* share with other writers. I've been fortunate in my career, and I've benefitted from several people like that. I've profited from their generosity. They're one of the reasons I can write for a living.

With this in mind, I've started a Facebook group in that spirit. Its name?

Author Unleashed

Join me there. The group is pushing toward 3,000 strong now. Our motto is this: Dig deep. Find the truth. Question standard practice – seek *best* practice.

Together, we're a group that shares knowledge among ourselves freely. It's a place to get feedback on blurbs and Amazon ads until they're honed to razor-like effectiveness. It's a place to discuss, discover and even drive the cutting edge of marketing for indie authors.

Want to be part of that? I look forward to meeting you.

Here we are. At the end.

I've talked a lot about business in this book. It is, after all, a marketing book. I've used terms like "prospect" instead of "reader". But don't be misled. I'm an artist. I love nothing more than to paint a picture with words. I think there's no nobler art than that of the storyteller.

But this book will be judged on its merits. It'll be judged by how well it did its job of giving you, the reader, information to help you on your writer's journey.

What I *hate* after reading a book like this is the feeling that it was stuffed with irrelevant and useless padding. What I *hate* is if the information I paid for was easily available elsewhere on blogs and the like.

If I've done those things to you, I deserve a review bomb.

On the other hand, if I've filled each chapter with good information that'll help you run Amazon ads, and I've given you a perspective on things that you haven't seen elsewhere, and most especially, if I've given you correct knowledge that will guide your labor, then I'd like to know that. Tell me in the reviews on Amazon. Tell me if this is a good book. Did I live up to my goal of giving you the information that will enable you to compete with the masses, even *outcompete* them?

What the experts say is that I'm supposed to insert a link here to make it easy for you to leave a review. They're not wrong.

But I'm not going to do that. You know how to leave one, if I've helped you.

The choice, as always, is yours.

Amazon ads are important. Maybe even critical if you want commercial success as a fiction writer.

But ads are only one piece of the puzzle. Ads bring visibility to your book. But what then? Having found a prospect willing to look at your book, is it a case of living happily ever after?

Is it *ever* a case of living happily ever after? No, it isn't. Or I'd have a lifetime supply of those marzipan brownies.

You still have to do the work. You still have to market. I've already covered blurbs in another book, but you need other sales copy than that.

And not just in the backmatter. Although that's important.

The next book in this series is about sales copy, other than blurbs. It's about how experts write it, and where they use it. Some of the information I reveal in that book will shock you.

I promise.

And it'll help you sell more books too. It helps me sell books. And in ways other writers without a professional copywriting background don't know or understand.

As with this book, I leave no stone unturned, and I give you that correct knowledge you need. The book will cover topics no other indie author does, and show you how to use sales copy in ways you've never considered and in places that'll raise your eyebrows like Spock on the bridge of the *Enterprise*.

Interested? Fascinated, even?

Anyway, thanks for reading. And as always, keep digging for the truth!